NICOLA MACDONALD is a Mum who worked in the marketing world. From her teenage years upwards, she discovered postpartum anxiety after her first child and was compelled to train as a Mindfulness teacher for stress and anxiety.

Nicola lives near Bath with her husband and two young children. She grew up on a farm in Devon with three cats and a dog. If she is down there visiting family you'll probably find her on a beach. She was a diligent teen who also loved to have fun with her friends, dancing and singing along to 90s music whenever possible.

Nicola runs courses for teenagers, adults, and the workplace (online and face to face). Check out bathmindfulness.co.uk for details. Nicola is also available for speaking events.

RESILIENT TEEN

Nicola MacDonald

SilverWood

This edition independently published in 2020

SilverWood Books Ltd
14 Small Street, Bristol, BS1 1DE, United Kingdom
www.silverwoodbooks.co.uk

Copyright © Nicola MacDonald 2020

The right of Nicola MacDonald to be identified as the author of this work has been asserted in accordance with the Copyright, Designs and Patents Act 1988 Sections 77 and 78.

All rights reserved. No part of this publication may be reproduced, stored in a retrieval system, or transmitted in any form or by any means, electronic, mechanical, photocopying, recording or otherwise, without prior permission of the copyright holder.

ISBN 9798655549234 (KDP paperback)

Page design and typesetting by SilverWood Books

Contents

Acknowledgements 7

Introduction 9

Part 1 15

    Chapter 1 – The basics of mindfulness 17

    Chapter 2 – School and the pressure to do well 27

    Chapter 3 – When friendships are rocky 37

    Chapter 4 – Accepting yourself as you are in mind and body 43

    Chapter 5 – Sitting with your pain 53

Part 2 57

    Chapter 6 – Handling life's pressures 59

    Chapter 7 – Bullying 66

    Chapter 8 – When life at home is turned upside down 76

Chapter 9 – A healthy approach to managing anger	82
Chapter 10 – Handling the ups and downs of dating	91
Chapter 11 – Social media	96
Chapter 12 – Handling illness or grief	104
Chapter 13 – Building deeper connections, truly being there for each other	110

The Meditations — 115

The Body Scan	117
The Breathing Meditation	122
The Mountain Meditation	125
Self-acceptance meditation	128
Mindful self-compassion	132
Mindful Movement	135

Glossary of terms — 147

Acknowledgements

To all at Silverwood Books who brought this book to life with such enthusiasm, thank you.

To Martina, thank you for going above and beyond to turn my jumbled up chapters into a flowing book.

To Kate, thank you for sharing a personal story with me that added more depth to my book.

To Karen, thank you for your training and support, the retreat was a real eye-opener that I will never forget.

To my parents and sister, thank you for your love and support. To mum and Hannah, thank you for the childcare, marketing ideas, and excitement at each stage of the publishing process. To dad and my late grandad 'Pop', thank you for introducing me to the beauty of nature, even if it meant a 'quick' trip to Exmoor to see the lavender on a windy, rainy day. Or getting up early to go and see wild deer in the fields.

To my friends, mother in law Rachel, sister in law Nerissa, Vicky, Andy, Bruce, and Lloyd thank you for your love and support. Special thanks go to Faye, Nat, Emma, and Nerissa for ideas, information, special writing journals, and marketing help.

To Sarah, thank you for always inspiring me to be myself. I imagine you smiling right now.

To my son and daughter, my life would be incomplete without you. Your infectious smiles brighten every day, thank you.

To my husband, without you, this book wouldn't exist. Thank you for supporting me on this journey. From the beginning of an idea right through to my training, another baby, and finally a book. You were busy behind the scenes looking after the kids as I wrote and went on training courses. Thank you for believing in me.

Introduction

Izzy isn't listening. Grace is chewing her pen. Cara is scanning the room to avoid my eyes. Blake is sneaking a look at his phone. I lost them when I mentioned breathing. I'd known that would be where I'd lose them. So, I bring their attention back with the Body Scan. Something clicks with this meditation. They lie down on the floor on mats, with some distance between them. Enough to avoid any prodding. A phone goes off. I remind everyone again to switch their phones off for 15 minutes. I see a look of relief in some of their eyes. Silence. Eyes closed. Bodies resting. No distractions. Nowhere else to be. No Snapchats to check out. No TikToks to learn. Silence. The sniggering stops. I guide them through the meditation. Grace stops fidgeting. Blake stops making jokes. After 15 minutes they're still quiet. I gently tell them it's the end of the meditation. Sounds slowly return to the room. But these sounds are different, gentle, considered. Some let out a sigh. Some give me a big smile as they stretch. Izzy says "That was lush". Cara says "I just felt the stress coming out of my fingers". Blake asks "Can we do it for longer next time?"

Mindfulness is a powerful thing. It slows things down for a while, reduces the busyness of the mind. This generation's teenagers need that more than ever. You have all the typical teen challenges of previous generations – school stress, friendship angst, family fall outs, body changes. But layered on top of that is the suffocation of social media that only this generation of teenagers can truly understand. Every 'like' is a form of validation, every Snapchat conversation is a chance to remain part of the group, every TikTok is a challenge to remain 'with it'. Your heartbeat reacts to this fast-moving social media world. It is so hard to keep up. Teenage anxiety is increasing and it's not hard to see why. And what about your self-esteem? You may not realise it, but just as any validation can give you a high, any form of disregard can give you a low…you know, those times when you've perfected that photo only for it to be ignored. Social media, and everything else that goes with being a teenager, can take a toll on your self-esteem unless you take steps to take care of how you feel inside. Being mindful will help you to learn how to notice when stress or anxiety are creeping in and how to take steps to handle them in a healthy way.

You see, I was an anxious teenager back in the 90s, before social media even existed (!!!). Stuff happened to me that wasn't unusual for a teen. I was bullied. I shouldered a lot of school pressure. I fell out with my friends. My parents divorced. I had boyfriend woes. Life was complicated. It took a toll on my self-esteem, robbed me of sleep and kept me in a state of agitation, ready to snap at anyone and anything in my path.

Tools like mindfulness were unheard of back then. So, I'm grateful that I can share the mindfulness tools I've learned over the years to help you meet the challenges of teenage life. To help you to become a more resilient teen.

What is mindfulness?

Mindfulness is about paying attention to the present moment. I mean the here and now. This second as you're reading this book. Not ten minutes before when you were Snapchatting or TikToking or whatever else you were up to.

I mean focussing all of your attention on an experience that you're having. It could be eating your favourite food…really savouring that chocolate spread on toast that smells like heaven and has your taste buds all aflutter. Sinking into every bite and noticing how your shoulders drop as you just melt into it. When you do this your mind is not fretting about an upcoming test or dwelling on an old argument with your dad from last week, it is focussed on one thing…the experience of the chocolate spread on toast. Don't get me wrong, your mind will have wandered off a little but, rather than indulging in thinking (playing out scenarios in your head), you will have guided it back to the present moment. You do this by connecting with your body and your breath. Here is another analogy to explain this…imagine you're at your favourite gig, absorbing every sound as it vibrates through your body, singing along to every lyric until your throat runs dry, feeling all the emotions that come with listening to music. And not reaching for your phone at any point to film it. Just being in the experience, not distracted by anything else around you. That's mindfulness.

How can mindfulness help you?

Mindfulness helps you to cope better with the external and internal challenges that you face every day. Practising mindfulness is like having a hidden superpower. It will boost your resilience the more you practice. Here's what The Blurt Foundation[1] has to say about resilience…

> "Resilience doesn't mean that you aren't affected by setbacks, rejection, or bad news. Resilience is about getting through, and dealing with, the negative events, and then picking yourself up afterwards…"

It is about surfing the waves of life one by one without getting sucked under. Mindfulness can help you to do this by equipping you with tools that help you to handle stress and anxiety whilst also boosting self-esteem. And the great thing is, it is available on demand. You can tune into your breathing and your body sensations whenever you want, wherever you want. No matter what is going on around you, mindfulness is there to help. I've used it when I've felt overwhelmed with emotions. I've used it to ground myself before giving a big presentation. I've used it in the middle of an argument to prevent my inner beast from exploding. I use it every day to help me balance my emotions in the face of life's chaos. I still have emotional wobbles, because that's part of being human. But, these days, my wobbles are more like mini rainstorms rather than full-scale tornadoes. The mindfulness techniques that I share in this book

1 The Blurt Foundation, 2019, https://twitter.com/BlurtAlerts/status/1135603 124142583809, @BlurtAlerts.

can be used every day to ground you in general or used 'on the spot' to ground you when dealing with specific challenges such as a bullying incident, a rejection, or a presentation in front of your peers.

How mindfulness works: Why do we react to things the way we do? Why can't we just 'keep calm and carry on'?

Before I discovered mindfulness, I used to question myself all the time. I kept judging myself for flaring up at the slightest thing. I knew that I struggled with stress and anxiety, but had no idea what was going on in my brain to cause that. I knew nothing about the brain. I now know a teeny tiny bit about the brain. I am definitely not an expert, so I apologise if this is a little too basic for you. I will explain what happens in the brain when the stress reaction kicks in so that I can then explain how mindfulness can intervene and help us to handle stress more effectively...

When we're calm, information is sent to the prefrontal cortex. This part of the brain is responsible for learning, thinking and reasoning. It controls our decision making and focuses our attention. Crucially, this is the part where we learn to read, write, analyse, predict, understand and interpret information. It is the part that you rely on a lot for school work!

When we're stressed the amygdala is ignited. This is a key player in the limbic (or feeling) system that controls our emotions and motivations. The amygdala is part of the 'lizard brain' which developed over 600 million years ago before the evolution of thoughts and emotions. Often known as 'fight or flight' or the 'alarm bell', it is our inbuilt survival mechanism that looks out for and protects us from things that can harm us. It was very useful two hundred thousand years ago when there were big scary predators trying to eat us for supper!

Today, we all still have that primal instinct of the amygdala. We can still see most things in life as a threat. The slightest thing can trigger us. It could be a raised eyebrow from a teacher, a group of teenagers sniggering in the back of class, a funny look from your sister's friend in the year above, etc. The amygdala will still fire off to prepare your body for imminent danger. Adrenaline and cortisol (the stress hormones) are released via the pituitary gland, increasing your heart rate and constricting your blood vessels. This causes your blood pressure to rise and anxiety to appear.

This then blocks information from passing through to the prefrontal cortex, that rational part of the brain responsible for decision making! Instead of rational decision-making, all of the incoming stimuli are processed through the automatic reflexive response of fight, flight or freeze.

Here's where mindfulness comes in. We humans have created this method that helps us to pause. When we pause, we trigger the parasympathetic nervous system, the 'rest and digest' system, which slows down and puts the brakes on our primal urge to react in fight, flight or freeze mode. When we practice mindfulness, the 'rest and digest' system says to the body, *"Hey, everything is ok, heart rate can slow down, sweat glands can chill, shoulders can relax"*. We have given ourselves the ability to respond rather than react to the situation we're facing.

Becoming a more resilient teen

There are two parts to this book. Part 1 introduces you to the longer-term practice of mindfulness, helping you to become more resilient. It introduces all of the longer meditations, the ones to do in the comfort of your own bedroom, and the ones that you can carry with you as part of your daily practice throughout life. Part 2 explains how to use mindfulness techniques to deal with specific instances in your life. In other words, using mindfulness 'on the go' to deal with challenging expected or unexpected situations.

Each chapter explores a different aspect of teenage life. However, any one aspect of teenage life may impact on others. Each chapter presents those challenges, and then invites you to practice a meditation. Some are 10 – 20-minute meditations to practice in your own safe space (bedroom, etc). The Centre for Mindfulness Research and Practice at Bangor University recommends that you meditate for 5 days out of 7. I know this may sound like a lot but the more you practice, the easier it becomes. Some are short meditations to use when you face a challenge and need a technique 'on the go' to ground you and give you a resilience boost. I recommend that you practice these at home too – as you encounter them in the chapters, so that you are prepared and know how to use them when you find yourself in a challenging situation out in the wider world.

Throughout the book I introduce a number of meditations for you to practice. These are all available for you to download via this link rebrand.ly/resilientteen. They are yours to keep, available to you whenever you need to access them. I recommend that you download all the meditations together so that you can easily access each one as and when you need it. The meditations vary in length from 10 to 23 minutes. As meditations are introduced in each chapter, you can listen to the accompanying audio file. However, depending on your circumstances, you may choose to read the book on its own without accessing the audio meditations or you may choose to combine the two. If you have the time and technology, I highly recommend that you listen to the audio meditations alongside this book to truly understand and benefit from the power of mindfulness.

I write about mindfulness through reflecting on my own teenage years. The book includes excerpts from my teenage diary, written in 1997 when I was 14 and 15 years old. I use those excerpts to reflect on what was going on in my life back then. The book also contains a few experiences from when I was an older teen, between the ages of 16 and 19, to add further depth to some topics.

I hope that the meditations, practices and techniques in the following chapters will help you to become a more resilient and mindful teen, ready to meet all of life's challenges.

Part 1

Chapter 1

The basics of mindfulness

Tuesday 9th September, 1997 – Back to school. I was afraid that everyone might have changed, but luckily, they're still the same. Everyone was being <u>really</u> nice, especially Jenny. The work isn't too hard <u>yet</u> and I got my homework done properly. We're all upset about Princess Diana dying.

These were the thoughts running through my 14-year old mind back in 1997. While the content has changed over the decades, anxiety about going back to school hasn't. In this day and age, it may look more like this…

Heart racing, chest squeezing, tummy flipping, armpits sweating…I'm lost in a film that is playing out in my head, a nightmare of worst-case scenarios. No-one will talk to me. Everybody hates me. My mates all have the same new haircut but I wasn't included in the Snapchat, so I'm stuck with my old look. The guy I like is now into my best friend. My new teachers think I'm stupid and are conspiring to take me down. My friends keep practising TikToks that I missed over the summer. I will say something stupid in Biology and everyone will laugh at me. I will have no-one to sit next to at lunch. The virus will come back after a month and we will be stuck at home again FOR ETERNITY.

So many reasons to fret about going back to school. And this year is a particularly strange one. You've had months of being trapped indoors away from your friends. MONTHS. Months of falling out with mum and dad and your siblings, if you have any. Months of fretting about this day…the day you go back to school. A rollercoaster of emotions flow through your body. Nervous energy that has you flitting between excitement and fear of what is to come. After all, fear and excitement are closely linked.

Are you making up stories about how it's all going to pan out? If so, just know this is normal. Our brains whizz around a lot of the time making up stories. Stories that grow in our heads, like we're film makers, directing an imaginary movie of our lives as they are going to happen. Some of us are so experienced at it that we can even add soundtracks and flashbacks. What we need to understand is that these stories are just that…stories. I know it can feel like they're real at the time…but they're not. They're simply a creation in our heads. We're very good at it. In fact, we're the masters of storytelling. And some of us can spend hours or even days building on our stories, adding further details, absolutely convinced that they're real. And the more time we spend indulging in our storytelling, the more those stories stir emotions within us, and the more out of touch with reality we become.

You see, fear likes it when we make up stories. They give fear a reason to stick around and cling to our shoulders like a leech, determined to suck any last remaining positivity out of us. It can feel like fear has taken over the control panel in our minds, determined to sabotage us in whatever way possible. But we don't want fear to take over, do we? It can stop us from doing things. It can hold us back from living a full life.

Choosing a different path

The thing is, we can accept that fear is there, but we don't have to let it rule our lives. Instead, we can choose to handle it differently. In fact, we can choose to handle all of our emotions differently. If we are prepared to learn, we can handle them in a healthier way. This book is all about helping you to handle the ups and downs of teenage life with tools that help you to cope with all sorts of challenges. Challenges that you're currently dealing with and those you may face in the future. After all, life is a rollercoaster of ups and downs. Nothing stays the same. Some days are full of ups…you smash your maths test, you catch the eye of that fit girl in History class, you nail a TikTok move you're been practising for ages. Life is sweet. Then something comes along to knock you over. Maybe your dad refuses to take you to that party that everyone is going to. Or a teacher slams you for a bad grade in front of the whole class and you can feel your embarrassment rippling through the room. This is life. As Jon Kabat-Zinn says, *"You can't stop the waves but you can learn to surf"*.[2]

Life's waves will keep coming, one after the other. Sometimes, a wave gently washes against your legs and doesn't move you in any way. Other times, a wave will unexpectedly slap you in the face and, as you're only getting over the initial shock, another comes and slaps you again. Each wave is different but, more importantly, each one is unpredictable. Oh, if only someone could warn you and say, *"Watch out, something big is coming your way, so be prepared! Brace yourself for that argument with your mum! Brace yourself for that angry teacher who expects more from you! Brace yourself for the mood your sister will be in when you get home!"* Nope. Unfortunately, life doesn't work like that. We can't stop the waves but we can learn how to handle them better using mindfulness-based techniques. And this book will show you how. All I ask is that you give mindfulness a go. You may be surprised. It may just change your life in ways that you never imagined.

Just breathe

Just breathe. Simple isn't it? And yet, so many of us don't realise how useful conscious breathing can be. What do I mean by conscious breathing? I mean simply noticing how your body feels as you breathe in and out. What?! I know, you may be thinking 'this is not for me'. To be fair, when I first read about mindfulness, I also thought it was not for me. I thought, surely breathing isn't going to cut it! I breathe every day! What more is there to know? How wrong I was. Breathing is more powerful than you realise, if you really tune into it. I mean really pay attention to how it feels in your body. How about trying it right now? Let go of that urge to resist and give it a go? What have you got to lose? You're already reading this

---

2   Jon-Kabat-Zinn, Ph.D. 2004, *Wherever You Go, There You Are: Mindfulness Meditation for Everyday Life*, Piatkus, p30.

book because you want some help with handling stress and/or anxiety. Well, it starts with your breath. So, give it a try. Simply read the next paragraph, then put down the book and give it a go.

Close your eyes and pay attention to your breathing. Just notice where you feel the breath most naturally in your body. This could be in your tummy as it rises on each in-breath and falls on each out-breath. Try placing a hand on your tummy if it helps you. Or perhaps you feel it more in the chest area as you notice how it feels as your ribcage expands on each in-breath and contracts on each out-breath. Or maybe you feel it more in your nostrils as you pay attention to your breath flowing in and out. Some of you may even hear it flowing in and out of your nostrils. Some may not. The key is to keep connecting with how it feels in your body.

So, how was that? Your mind was racing around, right? That's perfectly normal. It's what minds do. Everyone's brain likes to race around. The more you practice tuning in to your breathing, the more you will anchor yourself in the present moment, away from all those racing thoughts. When you practice this, you're not stuck worrying about the future and you're not replaying the past over and over, you are truly in the present moment.

Can you notice anything different in your body? The breath alters with your moods, movements or thoughts. If you were feeling a bit stressed before you read this, your body may be feeling slightly different. This is very subtle. Or perhaps you didn't notice anything this time. There is no right or wrong, as each experience will be different. Some days you will find that you really tune into how your breath feels in the body and sometimes you may struggle. It can depend on what is going on for you at the time.

The message I want to share with you is that, no matter what life throws at you, your breath is always there to anchor you, to ground you in the present moment. I can't tell you the number of times I have relied on my breathing to steady myself in challenging moments. Guiding yourself back to the present moment using conscious breathing is the foundation of mindfulness. You can do this whenever your mind tries to drag you back into storytelling mode. As I said in the Introduction, when we're making up stories we have stepped out of reality and are playing a film in our heads. Have you ever imagined an argument before? I have. Many times! I have played an argument over and over in my head… *'If she said this, then I would say that, then she would say this, and blah blah blah.'* Has this ever helped me? No. Has an argument ever turned out like that in real life? No. Was I merely in a trance? Yes. Mindfulness helps us to notice when we're caught in storytelling mode and anchors us back in the present.

Often when we're making up stories based on fear it's because we're feeling 'stressed out'. We are all triggered by stress in different ways. It could be a raised eyebrow from a teacher, a funny look from your mum, an innocent comment from your friend that you've taken personally. All sorts of things can trigger our brains to start racing around, fretting about life. And yet, did you know that, in every situation, you have a choice whether to respond or react? I know it may not feel like it in the moment when you are about to give some knee-jerk reaction, when you want to scream or shout at your dad because he's asked you for the millionth time if you've revised for that test tomorrow or when your mum keeps pestering you to clean your room. But you really do have a choice every single day whether to respond or react.

Respond or react: It's your choice

Responding rather than reacting is simply about pausing and tuning into your breathing. This starts to turn down the body's natural fight or flight mode, that urge to either explode at someone or run a thousand miles in the other direction (sometimes we want to do both at the same time!). Instead, when we tune into our breathing, we ignite the 'rest and digest' system which says to the body *'Everything is ok, relax those shoulders, unclench that jaw, sweat glands take a chill pill'*. This can reduce the chances of blurting out a reaction that may cause more stress for you in the long run. You know what I mean, hurting loved ones with venomous words that you can't take back and which could lead to consequences such as…having your phone privileges removed (!!!!). So, every time you feel stress creeping over your body making you want to fight or flee…tune into your breathing to anchor you in the present moment. Thich Nhat Hanh, a wise monk, says, *"Feelings come and go like clouds in a windy sky. Conscious breathing is my anchor*".[3] Remember this phrase. It will help you in so many different scenarios.

As a teenager, you experience challenges every day. This might be small stuff, such as a bad hair day or a spot that won't leave your face. But then there's the big stuff. The stuff that feels relentless and so heavy on your shoulders. Situations that are totally out of your control, where you have no choice but to surf the waves. Maybe something in your home life is impacting everything else around you. Big stuff at home is likely to affect you. If you're going through something right now, at home or elsewhere, you'll benefit from coping strategies more than ever. Whatever you're dealing with, mindfulness can help. Because it's not just about conscious breathing, it's also about learning to release emotions in a healthy way. I can go for a run if I'm frustrated and the rage inside of me may be released…but this is only temporary. Most of the time my feelings come back to haunt me later in the day. This is because I was trying to use running as a distraction, and I am not fully addressing the pain, anger, hurt or frustration inside of me. Maybe I don't want to address those emotions and find out what unmet emotional need is truly running the show.

Identifying the unmet emotional need

We all have emotional needs and they vary from person to person. Some of us may need more independence, some of us may need more security. Often when our emotional need is not met, we can feel the stirrings of frustration taking over. Perhaps deep down we need to feel heard, loved, understood or accepted.

Our deepest emotional needs need to be identified and acknowledged. How do we do this? By meditating. I don't mean going '*hmmmmmm*' while crossing your legs and waiting to be lifted out of your body up into the clouds in a dream-like state. Nope. I mean the opposite. You're not trying to lift yourself anywhere. You're not trying to escape your emotions. Instead you're firmly sitting or lying with them. No running. No levitating. Just sitting. Or lying. Grounding yourself in the body and the moment.

3   Thich Nhat Hanh, posted 2019, '*Conscious Breathing*', https://thichnhathanh quotecollective.com/2019/09/06/conscious-breathing-thich-nhat-hanh/

Feeling all the sensations and emotions that are buried beneath the surface. This may sound scary, but trust me, by going a little deeper you can begin to understand yourself better, and start to release feelings that you may have buried so deep…feelings that may be influencing your thoughts and actions because you haven't fully addressed them.

There will be days when you really don't feel like meditating. Those are the days when you would benefit from it most. I've had those days. On days when I don't practice, I notice a change, as anxiety starts creeping back into me. Once I've meditated, I feel mentally stronger, ready to take on the world again. Jon Kabat-Zinn says, *"You don't have to like it; you just have to do it"*.[4] Meditation is not something that you use only when you feel stressed or anxious, it is a lifelong practice. Regularly practicing meditation is about topping up your resilience fuel tank so that you don't end up on the side of the road with an empty tank and no reserves to call on.

Before you begin

There are a few points to bear in mind before you begin to practice mindfulness meditation.

- Find somewhere comfortable at home where you can practice your meditation. You need a space where you're less likely to be disturbed, ideally away from distraction.

- If you share a room with someone, let them know that you're going to meditate or leave a note near you to ask them to not interrupt you. If you have an annoying sibling, perhaps ask a parent if they can support you by keeping your sibling busy while you meditate.

- Ideally, put noise-cancelling headphones on so that you can't hear any other noise around you. Most of the meditations provided alongside this book are between 10 and 23 minutes long. You will hear the sound of a bell to signal the end of the session.

[4] Jon Kabat-Zinn, 2013, *Full Catastrophe Living: How to cope with stress, pain and illness using mindfulness meditation*, Piatkus, p378.

- If you get distracted during the practice be kind to yourself. You can pause my recording or rewind a section that you misheard. Even five minutes of a meditation is better than nothing.

- If available, grab a blanket to keep you warm during the practice. Often during a practice your body temperature will drop, so it is important that you are as comfortable as possible.

- Sometimes we need to meditate elsewhere. There might not be any cushions or blankets available to add comfort. If that's the case, then ensure your temperature is comfortable. If you're too hot, such as sitting in the hot sun, or too cold, such as sitting in a draft, move to a more comfortable space. Otherwise, you will be distracted by your body attempting to regulate its temperature. Try to avoid all such distractions. After all, you have enough going on in your mind!

- Remember no-one is judging how you're meditating. This may sound odd to you but, when I first started meditating, I was so anxious that I kept questioning if I was doing it 'right'. I started to imagine my meditation teacher telling me I was doing it all wrong! As long as you're practising bringing yourself back to the present moment every time you notice your mind wandering, you are doing it right.

- Know that your mind will wander. This is natural. Use your breath to anchor you and bring your mind back to the present moment.

- Keep at it even when you feel boredom creeping in. The more you practice, the easier it will become.

- Even the busiest minds can slow down. That includes those of you who struggle to concentrate for longer than five minutes. Anyone can do it if they're willing to give it a go.

And remember, mindfulness is not some permanent magic where you wake up one day in a zen-like state and suddenly nothing bothers you. My friends and family would agree that I am certainly not zen-like at all times! After all, we all feel and we don't want to numb ourselves to the world, we just need to look after ourselves better. Some evenings when I reflect on my day, I realise that something happened that would have previously triggered a reaction in me. Past me (who hadn't yet discovered mindfulness) would have reacted emotionally. But, because of mindfulness, I handled the incident differently and I was proud of myself. Cue internal high five! This is the power of mindfulness.

The Body Scan

Let's begin with a mindfulness meditation called the Body Scan. This meditation helps you to connect with your body more, allowing you to notice where you are holding onto tension, and then helping you to release it. The body gives us early warning signs that we're feeling stressed. These signals may fly under the radar so much that we don't even notice them until they are screaming at us to slow down. In the past, I tried to ignore what my body was trying to tell me, hoping that the tension would go away. But stress doesn't work like that. For me, it persisted as headaches, insomnia, night terrors and shoulder pain, but it shows up differently in the body for each person. Understanding your body's signals can help you to look after yourself better, and can allow you to catch stress before it spirals out of control down the path of a serious physical breakdown, an emotional outburst or both.

Give yourself 15 minutes to do the Body Scan. Lie down on a mat or comfortable floor. You may want to cover yourself with a blanket or put on a warm jumper, so that you don't get cold. Starting at your feet, one-by-one, scan the different parts of your body. This means focussing your attention on each individual body part, noticing all the sensations that arise. This could be tingling, vibrating, or if certain body parts feel warmer or cooler. One way to do this is to imagine that you are shining a torch on one body part at a time, gradually working your way up your body from your feet. This helps you to focus on the present moment, as your mind is tuned to one body part at a time. This may seem alien to you if you struggle to connect with your body. It may take a bit of getting used to, but the more you practice, the easier it becomes.

You may notice some tension in your body. Whatever you feel, whether it is pain, discomfort, tiredness, remember to be kind to yourself. Say to yourself *'It is ok to experience this, whatever is here I will lie with it and let it be as I find it'*. In doing so, you may find that some areas of tension start to lift a little. However, I do not suggest that you actively try to release that tension, as this can only serve to tighten the body more as it starts trying to change what is happening. Remember, mindfulness is about non-striving, and learning to sit with discomfort or pain as it truly is.

The Body Scan helps you to connect with the body more. The first few times you do this you may notice your mind racing with thoughts such as *'This is boring'* or *'I need to revise'* or *'What would friend X think of me if he could see me now'*. This is all completely natural. Your mind is used to running at one hundred miles an hour on a treadmill, so it will naturally take a bit of getting used to. The meditation is available to download via rebrand.ly/resilientteen and read within the 'Meditations' section from page 115 to 146.

If you find lying still particularly tricky you may find the Mindful Movement meditation more useful. Mindful movement is another meditation practice that helps to ground you in the body. The one provided alongside this book involves gentle yoga movements and is 23 minutes long. You will need a mat and comfortable clothing to practice this meditation. The meditation is available to download via rebrand.ly/resilientteen and read within the 'Meditations' section from page 115 to 146.

Chapter 2

School and the pressure to do well

Monday 24th November, 1997 – Ok during the day. Am miserable now. I have got <u>tons</u> of coursework which I am trying to get on top of but finding it really hard. I really need some sleep.

Tuesday 16th December, 1997 – I feel so awful. I haven't done any coursework or revision or anything yet. I'm so naughty. I MUST do some tomorrow. I MEAN IT.

Monday 29th December, 1997 – Spent the day doing nothing. I can't believe I wasted one whole day. Went to a ball with Lucy and friends. £10 to get in. Everyone older. In a mood and feeling sick on way home.

Tuesday 30th December, 1997 – Did some cookery coursework. I thought I had plenty of time to revise for mocks but I don't and will just have to read through the notes. Tomorrow must get up fairly early and do loads of coursework. Finish? I think not!

Wednesday 31st December, 1997 – Did hardly anything today…

How can it feel when the pressure of school becomes too much? Like you're on a rollercoaster with no end in sight. I don't mean that in a good way. I mean you're climbing up and up, working relentlessly to complete a piece of coursework, then you complete it and you whizz down the rollercoaster only for another piece of work to be required at the bottom. Then you start climbing again, completing sections as you go, and then whizz down for more work to greet you at the bottom again. The requirements can feel non-stop. It can be incredibly overwhelming if you think about it too much. You question if you have enough time to finish everything and yet, somehow, the work usually gets done in the end.

As a teenager, you're at a stage of life where expectations are high. So many people around you want the best for you and often, owing to the culture we live in, the best is seen as a life of wealth, power and status. And often grades are seen as the ticket towards that success. The pressure to do well at school is huge. That pressure may come from a few well-meaning teachers who see your potential, or from parents or grandparents who want more for you than they had. Wherever it comes from, that pressure can mount. It can feel like a huge weight on your shoulders. It can feel like you're striving all the time. Striving for that perfect grade in each subject, for that medal in gymnastics, for that certificate in ballet, for that place at the prestigious football academy you always dreamed of. The list goes on.

But mindfulness is non-striving. I don't mean that you give up on all your dreams and just sit in your garden all day long meditating! The world doesn't work like that. Mindfulness is a tool to help you to handle stress and anxiety, not a tool to opt out of life altogether.

Planning for your future is essential. What mindfulness gives you is a way to anchor yourself in the present moment when you get stuck worrying about the future too much. It is natural to worry about an upcoming exam, or a presentation you have to give, or a first date. In those scenarios your nervous energy centres around something specific. But when worrying starts to become more generalised, that is when anxiety may be creeping in. An example of this could be *"I'm really worried about my geography exam. If I don't get the mark I want, I'll never become a success in life. I'll end up living with my parents forever. Then they'll disown me and I'll live alone with cats for company and no-one will visit because I'll be an embarrassment."* Anxiety can be very debilitating and it can affect us in many ways. We can end up second guessing ourselves and overthinking every decision as we grapple with the multiple 'what ifs' rippling through our heads. From a body perspective, we can end up with numerous ailments, such as a tightened chest, muscle tension (shoulders, neck, back) and an increased heart rate that feels as if your heart is going to explode. While certain parts of our bodies can feel besieged, we can also struggle to connect with other parts of the body as the mind races around. It is an unpleasant experience that can leave you with a feeling of hopelessness.

If you're worried or anxious, you're not living in the present moment. Instead, you are preoccupied with thoughts of the future. Mindfulness helps you to pause and observe what is happening in the here and now rather than immediately reacting to a situation, and letting things spiral out of control. It helps you to recognise and catch your negative thought patterns before they really take hold, trapping you in a spiral of worry or anxiety. If you become aware of these thought patterns you can then choose whether to believe them or not. You can learn to consciously respond rather than react.

Breathing efficiently

When we pause and tune into our breathing, we are stimulating the rest and digest system, turning down the stress response (fight or flight mode). Have you ever noticed that when you feel overwhelmed with stress, your breathing is faster than normal? Fast and shallow breathing is also known as hyperventilation, where breathing is focussed more on the chest, back and shoulder regions. This is tiring for the body as it was not designed to work that way.

The diaphragm is the large muscle that sits in a curved position between the chest and the abdomen. When we breathe in, the diaphragm contracts causing the curve to flatten and displacing the internal organs which makes the abdomen expand. When we breathe out, the diaphragm curves upwards, creating more space in the abdomen for internal organs to move back to their previous position. This in turn flattens the tummy, pushing air out of the lungs. Why am I going into detail here? Because it helps to understand what happens in the body when we breathe efficiently and it can make a huge difference to your breathing technique. Abdominal breathing takes some practice and

I am not suggesting that you have to be an expert abdominal breather to benefit from mindfulness. Consciously breathing or tuning into your breathing is what matters the most, whether you notice the breath flowing more in your chest or your tummy. To practice breathing more efficiently, here is a breathing exercise to try. Why not give it a go?

Exercise to find your natural breath

This mindfulness exercise pays attention to the way you breathe. Practise it at home at a time when you are unlikely to be interrupted. As you practice, you will find that your mind starts to race off. Perhaps it wants to plan the next piece of work that's due or you start worrying about an imminent exam. It is natural for the mind to do this, it is used to being on the treadmill, working fast. So, if a thought pops up that takes you away from the present moment, try labelling it, then tune in to your breathing to anchor yourself back in the here and now. For example, it could be a recurring thought about a future exam so try labelling it as '*worrying*', or a long to-do list that keeps pestering you so try labelling it as '*planning*'. In this way you're fully acknowledging the thought, making a mental note as if to say, 'I will look at that later'. And so, to your breathing.

- Sit comfortably on a chair in an upright position with your shoulders relaxed, feet flat on the floor and your hands resting comfortably on your lap.

- Loosen any tightness in your clothing so that your tummy can freely rise and fall.

- Close your eyes and lower your chin towards your chest.

- Slowly and gently perform a mini body scan, focussing on each body part one at a time. Start by focussing all of your awareness on your feet, noticing how it feels to have all four corners of the feet firmly planted on the floor. Then slowly move your awareness up the back of your calves, gently travelling up to the knees, and then the thighs, right up to your buttocks on the chair. Pay attention to how it feels to be supported by the chair as you ground yourself here in this moment, in this practice, as you move your awareness to your lower back, creeping up to the middle of your back, all the way up to the top of your back, and finally taking in your shoulders. Then focus your attention on your hands, noticing any tingling or vibrations here, move to your elbows, forearms and upper arms right up to your shoulders again. Then travel up the neck, along the back of your head and finally, the top of your head. Be aware of the whole of your body sitting there breathing.

- Now let your attention drop into wherever you feel the breath most naturally.

- Notice how the breath ebbs and flows in its own rhythm.

- Notice any other sensations in the body as you sit there.

- Place one hand on your chest and the other hand on your tummy with your fingers resting above your belly button.

- Become aware of how your body feels on each in-breath and each out-breath.

- Notice if your hand lifts on your in-breath and gently drops on your out-breath.

- Perhaps one hand rises more than the other.

- Don't try to change anything, just be with whatever flows naturally.

- If your mind becomes restless, take it back to your breathing.

- Bring your focus back again to how it feels to breathe in your body.

- Now bring the focus back to your hands, keeping the hand that is moving the most on the body and dropping the other hand to rest on your lap.

- Keep the other hand where it is (either your chest or belly) as you stay with the rhythm of your own breath.

- Now gently lower your chin and slowly open your eyes.

- Take a few stretches to end the practice.

As you complete this practice ask yourself some questions… What was your experience? Where was your hand? Did it alter your experience of breathing? This practice will help you to understand your breathing better. I recommend also trying this while lying down, as you will see the belly rising and falling more easily.

Revising for exams

Breathing exercises, like the one above, are particularly useful for grounding yourself in the midst of stressful periods of school work. Exams are one of the most stressful times of your life. Even now, when my husband is stressed with work, he has nightmares in which he is back at school sitting down for an exam he hasn't prepared for.

It is extremely important that you take time to look after yourself during this key time of life, during both revision time and on the day of the exam itself. What you need is a healthy way to release the stress so that it doesn't bubble up and become too much. You don't want to end up burning out.

It is useful to pay attention to what happens in your body as stress hits. Your fight or flight reaction has kicked in, causing a surge of adrenaline and cortisol (the stress hormone) to start pumping around the body. Muscles start to tense, the heart starts pounding, blood pressure rises, sweat glands are activated, and much more besides. A lot is going on in the body as it prepares itself to fight or flee the situation.

For me, I often felt the stress of exams in my shoulders. They would start to tense, lifting up closer and closer to my ears. Then my mind would start whizzing through quotes and facts and random knowledge that wanted to come out. Or, in some cases, my mind would appear to go blank, as if I had lost all the information stored in my memory, tumbleweed blowing through my brain as I tried to recall everything. This is because when our fight/flight reaction kicks in, the prefrontal cortex, that part of the brain responsible for learning and decision-making, is affected.

Mindfulness intervenes by stimulating the 'rest and digest' system which turns down our stress reaction. As things slow down, energy is retained and the heart rate normalises. Information is sent to the prefrontal cortex, helping you to remain calm and focussed. You can then consciously respond to the situation rather than reacting to it.

In Chapter 6, I will introduce you to mini breathing exercises to specifically help you during the stressful exam season. These techniques will help you handle the stress of revision and stress in the moment (when you're sitting in the exam room about to start). Chapter 6 also explores other short techniques that you can use on the spot when you're feeling stressed at school, such as during an incident of bullying, when you're about to give a presentation or if you're asking someone out on a date.

Chunking

Sometimes when we feel overwhelmed with the enormity of the work piled on our shoulders, we struggle to see how we can get it all done. In our heads, the work becomes an insurmountable mountain. I would often indulge the thought that my work was never going to get finished. I can recall a specific example that still plays out in my mind to this day. I was working on a Geography school project that I couldn't seem to finish. There always seemed to be another section to complete. Anxiety was creeping in and I was making up a lot of stories in my head. I was fixated on the end product and the end grade and 'what ifs' were repeatedly popping into my head… *'What if I don't get the grade and don't get into a good school and what will my parents think of me'*, and other such thoughts. I ended up working way too much on that project but in a very unproductive way. In the end, I had so much detail that my teacher had to intervene and show me how to approach the project more mindfully. She took all my pieces of paper and used paper clips to break the project down into chunks. Pointing at different sections, she'd say "You do this, and then you do that". She encouraged me to focus on one thing at a time and she showed me how to divide the work out over the next few weeks. I am very grateful that my teacher was able to help me like that. Not everyone has a teacher with spare time to sit down and help you to chunk your workload.

By using a breathing technique before you start any big, seemingly insurmountable or never ending, piece of work, you will be able to approach it more mindfully.

Receiving feedback

Ugh. Feedback. Just the word makes my shoulders tense up and my jaw clench. It doesn't matter whether its feedback from a teacher or what your parents say about how you're progressing at school, the idea of feedback can fill us with dread. Here is a little anecdote from a friend of mine…

My friend wrote an academic book and sent it to the publisher in 2014. She received a borderline rejection – they'd accepted it but only if she put in major work. The three reviewers all gave her very long and detailed feedback. She read the first page from the editor, and put it in a drawer. And never did anything more with the book. You know when she eventually read the reviewers' comments? – and this is the truth – six years later. And guess what? The comments weren't that bad. Some were really bad. But there was some really positive stuff in there too. It had taken her 6 years to pluck up the courage to pick up her book again and carry on.

Did you know that our brains have negativity bias? I find this fascinating. According to Rick Hanson, psychologist and author of *Buddha's Brain*, our brains are hardwired to scan the environment for bad news[5]. This is owing to 600 million years of evolution and our ancestors watching out for predators to avoid getting eaten. We have retained this negativity bias in our brains and, as a consequence, we

5   Rick Hanson, Ph.D. with Richard Mendius, MD, 2009, *Buddha's Brain: the practical neuroscience of happiness, love and wisdom*, New Harbinger Publications, Inc. p68.

more readily store bad news than good news. Bad news sticks in the head like Velcro in a matter of seconds. This helps to explain why, when we receive feedback, we tend to remember one negative comment rather than a whole lot of positive comments. Positive experiences, on the other hand, require at least 20 seconds of attention to be stored/absorbed into the memory. As a result, we don't spend enough time appreciating the good and, instead, naturally focus on the bad.

Mindfulness can help us to handle feedback better. The next time you receive feedback, rather than attacking yourself with all the negative comments that hurt you, how about trying a meditation when you get home? The Breathing Meditation will help to calm your mind and release tension in the body. After you have meditated you may find that you remember some of the positive points as well as the negative points. A more balanced frame of mind can help you to store news as a neutral pathway or a positive pathway in the brain rather than as a purely negative pathway, as you may have done in the past. The meditation is available to download via rebrand.ly/resilientteen and read within the 'Meditations' section from page 115 to 146.

As for handing feedback on the spot, turn to Chapter 6 to learn about shorter mindfulness techniques to keep you grounded and balanced.

Mountain Meditation

Practising the Mountain Meditation can help you to remain grounded as you prepare for the day ahead. It can give you the confidence to face any challenges coming your way – an exam, a chat your teacher has scheduled, the social stuff you have to face at school.

This is a 10-minute meditation that you can practice in the morning before going to school. I find it useful as a grounding tool and a confidence boost. You learn to root yourself to the ground regardless of what is going on around you. As with a mountain, you are unshakable, solid and unmoved by the changing weather patterns around you. Mountains endure unpredictable hits of weather on a regular basis. Sometimes they are covered in a blanket of snow, sometimes they are slapped in the face by hail, sometimes they are pushed by unrelenting winds. Whatever the season, they remain solid, rooted in the Earth's crust. As Jon Kabat-Zinn explains, "...*we can embody the same unwavering stillness and rootedness in the face of everything that changes in our own lives over seconds, hours and years...*"[6]

Take inspiration from the mountain. Yes, there are often other voices circling around you, sometimes uninvited, providing their opinions. Remember that those voices will pass just as the weather and seasons will pass. Those voices don't reflect your true self. They are the voices of other people's perceptions of you and of life in general. You are your own person with your own experiences and your own views of the world. Try not to get caught up in those icy winds that threaten to push you over or that relentless hail that makes you want to hide away in a cave for days at a time. Other people's voices are merely the wind and rain that will pass by. You can blow them away in a meditation, blowing out the tension that diminishes you. You are capable of so much.

How about giving the Mountain Meditation a go? The best time to listen to this meditation is in the morning before you go to school, especially as you prepare to give a presentation, take a test, or something else where you need to feel grounded to the Earth. If you don't have time to practice this meditation in the morning, try doing it the night before. If you have time, listen to it twice – once in the evening and again in the morning. In fact, the more you listen, the more your self-esteem takes a boost. The meditation is available to download via rebrand.ly/resilientteen and read within the 'Meditations' section from page 115 to 146.

The techniques provided in this chapter can help you have a more positive school experience. Breathing exercises can help you to handle the stress and anxiety that comes with mounting school pressure, anchoring you in the present moment whenever it feels like too much. The Mountain Meditation can help to prepare you for any challenge coming your way, rooting you to the ground regardless of what others may say or do around you. Whatever circumstances you may face at school, mindfulness will anchor you time and time again.

---

[6] Jon Kabat-Zinn, Ph.D. 2004, *Wherever You Go, There You Are: Mindfulness Meditation for Everyday Life*, Piatkus, p138.

Chapter 3

When friendships are rocky

Tuesday 9th December, 1997 – Lara has blanked me today. I ask her what's wrong and she always says 'nothing'. I get really frustrated with her. I don't have a clue what's the matter with her. She tries to prove that she is happier with others by always laughing with them.

Wednesday 10th December, 1997 – Lara has still blanked me today. It was the school parties today. Did no work. What fun. What a relief. In the Talent Contest I did Barbie Girl with others. It was great fun.

Thursday 11th December, 1997 – Lara was really chummy with Claire all day long. I found out that she is worried that Lucy is taking me away from her and that she will split us up. Luckily, at the end of the evening after the Carol Service we were friends.

How does it feel when your friends ignore you? You may feel lonely… lost…even a little vulnerable. You may start to make up stories in your head that everyone is laughing at you behind your back. You may even make up stories to explain their behaviour, assuming that you have done something 'wrong' to cause this treatment. After all, your brain is wired to be part of the friendship group. You can't help it; you have biology to thank for it. According to Sarah-Jayne Blakemore, studies have proven that during our teenage years friends are more important to us than at any other stage of life.[7] Every ounce of your being yearns to be included. To be part of what's going on. You want to be in on the 'in jokes', not left out in the cold, feeling eyes on you, hearing whispers around you. So, when you feel disconnected from friends it can feel as if a dark cloud has fallen over all aspects of your life. Everything can feel a bit 'meh' and everyone around you (especially parents) can trigger you to react by blurting out something hurtful as a result of this misery. You certainly don't feel or behave like yourself when friendships are rocky.

We've all heard of FOMO, the fear of missing out. But I also think FOBLO – the Fear of Being Left Out – is just as important. Fear of being left out from social invitations in the first place. My friend can still recall the 'devastating' moment as a teenager when she walked into town with her mum and spotted her friendship group out shopping without her. They hadn't invited her along on the trip. It was unlucky that she saw them as, back when we were teens, we didn't have social media (!!!) so we wouldn't always know if friends were catching up without us. Nowadays, teens face the opposite scenario. The over-sharing nature of social media means that you see pretty much everything that goes on. You could easily spot a post from a night out that you had no clue about. It is one thing to miss out on events because of homework, strict parents or a nasty cold, but it is far more hurtful if you haven't even been invited in the first place, and have been left out entirely. This can create all sorts of stories in your head as to why you weren't invited. 'Was it because I was too friendly with that girl she liked? Was it because I laughed at that teacher's joke when the others didn't find it funny? Was it because I didn't join in when they were picking on that girl at lunch?' These sorts of stories build in your head as you start to convince yourself that they're real.

Become an observer of your thoughts

Mindfulness can help you to notice when your mind is racing, when it is indulging in overthinking, when it is running its own rumour mill or

---

7   Sarah-Jayne Blakemore, 2019, *Inventing Ourselves: The Secret Life of the Teenage Brain*, Penguin Random House UK, Transworld Publishers Ltd, p31.

pretend film. The more you practice meditation, the more you can become aware of how your mind behaves. You become the OBSERVER of your thoughts rather than feeling like their victim. How can you become the observer of your thoughts? Here is a great analogy to explain how…

Imagine you are sitting on a riverbank. Close your eyes and picture yourself there. The stream flowing past you represents your mind and the leaves carried on the current are your thoughts. Each leaf is different in size, colour and shape, just like all your thoughts are different. After all, random thoughts enter our heads all the time. We can flit between planning what we'll do at the weekend, to what a teacher said to us yesterday, back to what we'll wear on Saturday, then back to *'Is it time for lunch yet'*. This goes on and on…thought leaves appearing in the current of your mind.

In this scenario you have a choice. You can choose to jump into the stream and get caught in it…indulging in the thought, allowing it to build in your head and make up further stories to support that first thought. Or, you can choose to merely observe your thought stream from the riverbank, without judgement.

We can spend a lot of time adding judgement to the thought stream. We are so hard on ourselves, aren't we? *Ugh, why do I feel like this? Why am I worrying again? Why can't I stop thinking about X?* No wonder we can so easily get lost in our thoughts, and then lost in thoughts about our thoughts!

This may seem impossible to you right now but, trust me, with practice you can learn to merely observe your thoughts without judgement. The first step towards settling the mind is simply sitting and breathing with your thoughts, allowing them to float by one by one without picking on yourself. The reality is, the more you sit and breathe, allowing these thoughts to pass by (practising meditation regularly), the easier the stream will flow.

You will find that some thought leaves get stuck, caught in a whirlpool, a loop of thinking. Perhaps you're judging others, then judging yourself for judging others, then feeling unworthy, then wondering why, and getting caught in the past. This is natural and is no reason to beat yourself up. When you are caught up in thinking (where your mind is either in the future or the past), use your breathing to guide yourself back to the present. As you are learning from this book, breathing is your anchor. It is your home base. It grounds you. Your mind will regularly drift off, so mindful breathing will become your best friend.

If the riverbank analogy doesn't appeal to you, try thinking about the clouds in the sky. This concept is similar to the riverbank analogy, where your mind is represented one way, and your thoughts in another. However, in this scenario, your mind is like the sky, vast and endless. Now imagine your thoughts as clouds coming and going. Some are big, some are small. All are different. Let your thought cloud come along, stay for a bit and then pass by. By acknowledging it you have given some time to it but then let it pass by as it is meant to. When I refer to acknowledging your thoughts, I mean labelling them. If a thought arises where you're judging a friend about something that he said or did, try labelling it as '*judging*'.

Learning to not take things personally

Mindfulness can also help you to notice when you're taking things personally. As you become the observer of your thoughts, you begin to see the bigger picture more often, to understand what is really going on, rather than the story you're telling yourself. Imagine you see a friend across the street on the walk to school. You wave at her and she sees you, but doesn't wave back. You feel hurt and embarrassed. Judgemental thoughts and stories start to creep into your head... '*How rude... She doesn't like me anymore... Does she think she is better than me?*' You see her in class later in the day and you act differently towards her. She notices this and acts differently with you. This discomfort between you might go on for days or even weeks!

The reality is you don't know the context behind her behaviour, or the circumstances that led her to ignore you this morning. You don't know that she was dealing with some devastating news about a family member, preoccupied with her own thoughts and feelings. She wasn't fully paying attention to what was going on around her. Had you known this, you would have empathised with her situation and not taken things personally. This can happen a lot in life where we play out stories in our heads to try and explain other people's behaviour when the real reason may be entirely different.

Mindfulness can help us in a situation such as this. Now, imagine that scene again… You notice a friend on your way to school, you wave at her, she sees you but doesn't wave back. You feel hurt and embarrassed. Judgemental thoughts and stories pop into your head… *'How rude… She doesn't like me anymore… Does she think she is better than me?'*

This is the point where mindfulness can intervene. If you have been practising mindfulness regularly, your brain will notice more quickly when it's about to get caught up in a rumour mill of its own making. You pause. You take a conscious breath. You label what your mind is up to, and say to yourself '*judging*'. You pause again and take another conscious breath, gathering yourself and perhaps acknowledging any emotions that have surfaced due to the unreturned wave, such as 'embarrassment' or 'sadness'. You say to yourself *'Maybe she is dealing with something…I hope she is ok'*. When you see your friend in class later, you notice that she has been crying. You give her a hug and listen to her suffering.

When we're caught up in taking things personally, we struggle to find perspective. We struggle to see what is really going on as we're stuck in victim mode. Mindfulness helps us to view a situation differently with the eyes of an observer rather than a victim. We learn that sometimes when people act differently towards us it may not be personal; they may have something else going on in their lives that is causing them pain or discomfort. (Caveat – if someone is hurting you with no clear, understandable context behind his or her behaviour that is abuse and must be handled appropriately. Please speak to an adult you can trust.)

Friendships will chop and change

It is important to understand and accept that you can't control your friendship with another person. Sometimes friends may decide to hang out with other people for a while. This doesn't reflect on you as a person. It doesn't mean that, somehow, you're 'not good enough' or not worthy of them. It is simply how life goes sometimes. Nothing is permanent and friendships often switch around in the teenage years as people grow and change. Some friends may return to you later down the line. I have certainly found that. In the meantime, the best thing to do is make new friends. There are always other interesting people to get to know. Perhaps you dismissed them before with some form of judgement. Judgement can hold you back from building new relationships with people. If you can put aside some of your prior judgements using the techniques I have outlined above (pausing, labelling etc.) you may find that certain people you initially dismissed actually have the potential to be wonderful friends for you. I found this to be true as I made friends in my teenage years. I used to dismiss the quieter ones as 'not for me' as I wanted to be around the loudest people in the room. This was based on judgement that somehow the quieter types would be 'boring' and it wasn't true at all. Everyone is interesting if we learn to judge less and remain open to getting to know more people.

Mindfulness can help us in lots of ways when friendships are rocky. We can act more mindfully towards our friends by becoming the observer of our thoughts, identifying when our minds have wandered off creating rumours that aren't true. It can help us to understand that sometimes our friends may seem 'off' with us because something is happening in their lives that we're unaware of. We pause and consider the bigger picture, allowing us to take things less personally and accepting that we all have stuff going on in our lives. It can help us to embrace change as we learn to accept that relationships change over time. As Jon Kabat-Zinn says, *"You can't stop the waves but you can learn to surf"*.[8]

---

[8] Jon-Kabat-Zinn, Ph.D. 2004, *Wherever You Go, There You Are: Mindfulness Meditation for Everyday Life*, Piatkus, p30.

Chapter 4

Accepting yourself as you are in mind and body

Wednesday 12th February, 1997 – Had a bath. Did some theory. I wish my hair would stay the same thickness as it is wet. It always goes thicker when it dries. It's annoying. I went to the dentist. Can't wait til my teeth straighten.

Friday 14th February, 1997 – Had my hair cut. It looks terrible because she curled it and it went really thick. I straightened it and wore it down at the ball but it still looked awful. I took Sarah and Melz to a ball at the White Hart Hotel. It was good but I lack confidence major bad. I just couldn't talk to any boys there. James, Russell and Benji were all good looking.

Tuesday 1st April 1997 – Went to the dentist. I'm getting so annoyed with my teeth, I just want them to go straight! I've forgotten to do any April Fools on anyone.

Thursday 8th May 1997 – I keep having these thoughts that one day I will walk into school on a Monday telling everyone that I'm going out with Luke. I'm so thick sometimes. It won't happen. I wish it would. Been a science day – great! (sarky)

Friday 23rd May 1997 – Went camping with Sarah and Melz. We ate everything! I can't help acting a bit immature around them. I must stop!

These are just a few entries from my diary which suggest that I struggled with my self-esteem. There are many more entries that I could have used in this book. Emma Stone, in a lovely and very poignant way, says,

> "*I can't think of any better representation of beauty than someone who is unafraid to be herself.*"[9]

This may be a tricky question for you to answer but…do you accept yourself as you are? I mean every single part of you – your personality, your body, your face, your laugh? I imagine the answer to that question is probably no. And that's sad.

This could be down to all sorts of reasons…the culture you live in, how confident your parents are, how much time you spend scrolling through celebrities on Instagram, how body confident your friends are… and the list goes on.

So, let's start with friends…do you compare yourself with your friends? I imagine so. As a teenager you may feel a strong desire to be validated by your friends on a regular basis. This keeps you in the group and not out in the cold. As I've mentioned before, your brain is hardwired to be part of the tribe, so this is natural. What you may find hard is trying to remain yourself along the way. A desire for acceptance may lead you to change the way you look or behave in order to 'fit in' with the crowd. It may result in you losing a part of yourself along the way (perhaps that cute laugh that your mum loves or that silly dance that you do at home). Do you feel accepted or do you still feel a bit lonely and on edge? Friendship pressure is huge. And even when you have a ridiculous number of friends on social media you can still feel misunderstood or alone. Even the most popular teens I teach tell me that they can struggle to make deep connections with their friends. Social media has a lot to answer for. It can give other people the impression that we're happy and we've got our **** together. Yet a lot of us (even adults) can still lack true, deep friendships.

And then there are those of you who don't blend in with everyone else.

[9] Emma Stone, 2011, 'Emma Stone talks beauty secrets in The Help', https://www.youbeauty.com/beauty/emma-stone-talks-beauty-secrets-in-the-help/

Those of you who stand out from the crowd because you choose to adopt a different look from the majority. You may have a stronger sense of who you are than most your age. This is something to be proud of. And yet, whether you choose to acknowledge it or not, standing out from the crowd because you're 'different' can still take its toll on your self-esteem. Regardless of the mask you wear as you stroll into school, you can still be hit with feelings of loneliness and anguish. After all, acting or looking different can sometimes push you further out of a friendship group. You may even find that some of your friends have vanished as you've blossomed into your true self. This can cause such anguish as you are torn between the need to be yourself and the need to be part of a group. Even though you have chosen to show your difference it can be confusing and hurtful when others won't share your interests, or worse, call you '*weird*'. It can make you feel lonely in a crowd as you are ignored or, worse, picked on for not conforming. Sadly, the more you unearth your true self, the more alone you may feel. What a confusing emotional rollercoaster of a time. You may even choose to withdraw from your peers altogether, spending more time alone with your thoughts. And those may be fearful thoughts of the future, such as '*Will I ever make friends who accept me for me?*'…'*Will I always feel alone?*'…'*Will I always be seen as weird?*' or worse…'*Will I ever be good enough?*'

The answer to all of these questions is that you are absolutely good enough JUST AS YOU ARE. As you brace yourself to walk into school, skirting around a peer group until someone notices you, what you don't realise is a lot of your peers are doing the same. They're also bracing themselves before they enter the school gates. Even the most popular kids face self-doubt and fear. They also want to be included. To be part of the crowd. To be in on the 'in jokes', to not be left out in the cold, feeling eyes on them, hearing whispers around them. You are more than enough just as you are. Stand tall. Be proud.

External validation comes and goes

Seeking external validation is risky as it can change in an instant. One moment you may be the most popular person in school, and the next you have become the least popular. Frustratingly, you have no control over that. School can be harsh at times, a place that's deeply confusing, with a, sometimes, downright nasty display of mind games. At other times it can be pleasant and relatively drama free.

These ups and downs of school can have a knock-on effect on your self-esteem. One moment you feel good about yourself, the next you want to hide away in a hole for eternity. It can be hard to accept who you are when others are commenting on you or picking on others around you. It hurts to witness other people being targeted and it hurts even more to be targeted.

Even though the voices around you can change their tune in a heartbeat, you can remain true to yourself. Believe me, you can still be true to yourself. Amidst the teenage storms that rage around you, you can remain grounded. You can remain solid and rooted regardless of what other voices are saying or what other people are doing.

Understanding yourself better

How can you remain grounded and true to yourself regardless of the voices around you? By meditating. Meditating helps you to hear your true voice in amongst all the other voices whizzing through your head…you know, your friend's voice telling you to wear more make-up in order to be more 'attractive'…or your brother's voice telling you to stop listening to that band that everyone else thinks is 'lame'…or that girl you follow on Instagram telling you to only eat green food if you want to be popular.

As a teenager you have so many voices giving you advice on your life. How are you able to tune into your own voice? Meditation helps you to do this. By giving yourself some quiet time, away from all the distractions you face on a daily basis, quietening the racing mind so that you can listen fully to how you really feel about life.

This can take time. I'm not suggesting that the first time you meditate all the answers to life's questions will appear to you in your inner voice. If only! But I am saying that through practice you will come to know a deeper silence, and in that silence the answers to questions can arise. I find that sometimes I can spend days mulling over something – a big question that needs answering in my life. I then meditate, allowing all the other voices I've heard to pass by like clouds in the sky, and a strange knowing appears. The answer was there all along, hidden beneath the noise of other voices.

The more you meditate, the more of you is unlocked, allowing yourself to truly emerge. You start to get a better idea of who you are, amongst the crowd of voices that enter your head on a daily basis. Then you can begin to accept who you are, bit by bit.

Accept yourself – starting right now

YOU can validate yourself using mindfulness techniques. The more you validate yourself, the less you may seek validation from others. I'm not saying you will no longer care what people think. After all, your brain is geared in a certain way and it currently craves social acceptance. But you can still validate yourself. You can still boost yourself up as many times as you need to regardless of what is happening around you.

The Mountain Meditation that I introduced in Chapter 2 is a brilliant meditation you can use to boost self-esteem. It helps to ignite the 'rest and digest' system when you start to doubt yourself, when fear tries to make our legs wobbly or makes you want to pee yourself…or both.

The mountain inspires you to remain unmoved by the weather patterns around you. The voices around you will pass by just as weather and seasons inevitably pass by the mountain. These voices don't reflect your true self. You are your own person with your own experiences and views of the world. Try not to get caught up in those icy winds that threaten to push you over or that relentless hail that makes you want to hide away in a cave for days at a time. You can blow those voices away in a meditation, blowing out the tension that diminishes you. You are capable of so much. Resting all your self-esteem on what others think of you is a recipe for disaster. So, practice the Mountain Meditation to boost your self-esteem. Listen to it a few times to really take in the message that you are stronger than you think and more than enough just as you are. The meditation is available to download via rebrand.ly/resilientteen and read within the 'Meditations' section from page 115 to 146.

I'm asking you to start accepting yourself just as you are, deep down to the core. I mean every single part of you. As a teenager, it can be hard to accept yourself, but how about giving it a try. Let's start right now. Spend a few minutes considering your relationship with yourself. Do you have a good relationship with yourself? It sounds funny, but it is an important question. After all, your relationship with yourself is the most important one in your life. Do you like yourself? Can you list a couple of positive personality traits you have? If you struggle to feel warmth towards yourself, how about imagining what a good friend would say about you. Even just one or two traits will help to engage your brain to view yourself more positively. These baby steps are just the beginning. Can you write them down and put them by your bed? Humour me and give it a go. Writing yourself positive notes that you can read when you need to can have a big impact during moments of self-doubt or self-attack. They can remind you to be kind to yourself when things get tough.

Body image

How about your body…do you accept the body you have right now? I imagine the answer to that question is also no. Sad emoji. After all, Western culture is almost obsessive about how we look. Although society has progressed in ways, so that mental health is talked about more than it used to be, we still live in a society that idolises surface appearances. Advertising, social media and TV are rife with unhealthy and misleading messages around body image, such as '*Have this body and you'll feel better about yourself/become more attractive/get the attention you've been dreaming of*'. Sadly, it's all too easy for teenagers to internalise these unhealthy messages without even realising it and for those messages to continue to play out throughout your adult life.

What is seen as attractive often changes over time depending on the latest role models and the decade we're in. Trying to keep up with these constantly shifting goalposts is exhausting. Taylor Swift[10] said…

> "…There's always some standard of beauty that you're not meeting. Because if you're thin enough, then you don't have that ass that everybody wants, but if you have enough weight on you to have an ass, then your stomach isn't flat enough. It's all just ****** impossible."

10 Taylor Swift, 2020, *Miss Americana*, www.netflix.com, American documentary film directed by Lana Wilson.

She's right. But this isn't only an issue for girls. It can feel impossible for boys too. You just have to look at reality TV shows like Love Island to see that guys look different from the skinny dude on Shipwrecked when I was a teenager. Guys in the media these days are more beefed up than they used to be owing to more time spent at the gym and obsessive unhealthy habits to get that look. The pressure to look good is huge. You can easily start and end your day with negative messaging about your body filtering into your subconscious. Perhaps you don't have the more rounded bum that is 'in' at the moment, perhaps you don't have that washboard stomach like Chris Evans from Captain America. Comparing, comparing, comparing all day long. It is exhausting and draining and will naturally take its toll on your self-esteem.

On the plus side, some celebrities have wised up to this and use their fame to help boost other's self-esteem by embracing who they truly are behind the social media curtain. The baldness proud photography shoot led by Olivia Bentley sends positive messages around self-acceptance. The #Icrybecause campaign led by Tommy Mallett is another shift towards embracing yourself as you are by encouraging men to open up more.

These shifts towards self-acceptance are a start, yet we still have a long way to go. According to a recent online survey[11] by The Mental Health Foundation with YouGov, over one third of UK teenagers feel upset or ashamed of their body image and one in five UK adults have felt ashamed of their body image in the last year.

Most of us, adults included, can often feel as though we fall short in some way because we don't match up to the ideal body image projected all around us. Even adults can get stuck scrolling through Instagram, looking at famous people's faces or bodies and thinking, '*I would love to have that hair…or that body shape…or those eyes*'.

As a teenager, you can spend so much time picking at what you see as your flaws. I spent a lot of time criticising myself as a teen. I would look in the mirror and immediately pick apart my face and parts of my body I didn't like because I didn't look like a certain celebrity. My day

---

11   Mental Health Foundation, 2019, Body Image Report, https://www.mental health.org.uk/publications/body-image-report/exec-summary

would start and end with me being critical of myself. No wonder my self-esteem was low. My inner voice was criticising me before I even left the house.

Be compassionate to yourself

Mindfulness helps us to notice more quickly when we are attacking ourselves, when we're caught in a whirlpool of negative self-talk. With mindful awareness you can pay attention to what your mind is up to and catch that negative narrative before it spirals out of control. In fact, if you practice regularly enough, kinder thoughts can start popping into your head. For example, *'She has lovely hair…A hairdresser will have made it up like that…My hair is lovely too when I've just been to the hairdresser.'*

It is so important to pay more attention to how you speak to yourself internally. As Echart Tolle puts it, *"Every fragment of self-talk is a little story in the head that goes around, and then you look at reality through the lens of that little story"*.[12]

If you constantly tell yourself that you're not pretty enough/ muscly enough/toned enough then that story will grow in your head to the point where you have cemented it as absolute truth. You are effectively wearing ugly blinkers, unable to see the beautiful parts of you. You look in the mirror and all you see are the bits you want to change. It is a miserable situation to be in. You don't spend any time attempting to be positive and being more compassionate to yourself, with thoughts such as *'I have kind eyes'* or *'My body is strong'*… Instead you treat yourself to a barrage of self-abuse. This cycle will continue until you take a step back and start looking after your mind using tools such as mindful self-compassion.

When I discovered mindfulness, I learned to gradually accept myself as I am. In fact, *'May I accept myself as I am'* and *'May I be kind to myself'* are two key phrases that I use in the self-acceptance meditation that accompanies this book. I find it immensely helpful to say these phrases when I'm feeling a little low about myself. At first, it may feel cringeworthy

---

12 Eckhart Tolle, 2018, https://twitter.com/eckharttolle/status/1229900937961115654?lang=en

talking to yourself in this way but, trust me, over time your brain will benefit by building more positive neural pathways towards body acceptance. The meditation is available to download via rebrand.ly/resilientteen and read within the 'Meditations' section from page 115 to 146.

Mindfulness helps us to accept ourselves as we are and love ourselves as we are. Every single bit of ourselves. Yes, even the bits that you may currently despise. Even those bits. It is about learning to embrace yourself completely and wholeheartedly…perceived wobbly bits and all.

Being kind to yourself may seem unnatural at first but, the more you practice, the more natural it starts to become. After all, why do we show empathy for other people's suffering, yet not for our own? How often do we berate ourselves for not being 'good enough'? We are our own worst critics. We can easily fall into a spiral of negative thoughts such as *'I'm not good enough'*, *'Everybody hates me'* or *'I can't change anything'*.

Consider these questions: How much do you attack yourself? How strong is your inner critic? Do you accept yourself as you are, or are you constantly picking at yourself? Picking because you don't have the same hair as X at school, because you're not as funny as Y, because your girlfriend pays more attention to your PE teacher than to you, because you just can't get the highest mark in Geography, but consistently make second or third.

Your inner critic is not doing you any favours. You may think that the more you pick at yourself, the more successful you will be in life. Well, how do you measure success? Are you basing it on wealth? Power? Status? What about self-acceptance and good self-esteem? Even the wealthiest people in the world can suffer with mental health issues because they didn't look after themselves as they climbed the career ladder. With tragedies, such as the death of Caroline Flack, creating shockwaves across social media, we are reminded more than ever to take better care of ourselves. More famous people than we realise have suffered and are suffering from mental health issues. Emma Stone started receiving therapy for anxiety when she was only seven years old. Adele, Zayn Malik and Taylor Swift have all suffered from anxiety. The fact is, everyone needs to take care of their mental health, regardless of wealth or status or power.

Use inspirational quotes

Another way to boost self-esteem is by putting up quotes in your bedroom that inspire and comfort you. You may find some quotes provide more comfort than others, so find ones that work for you alone, in your unique situation. A quote that works for your friend may not work for you, and vice versa. If you need to keep it private, particularly if someone in the house is likely to pick it apart, then do so. Always protect yourself. There is no need to share everything if you don't want to.

It is really important that you start learning to accept yourself as you are. Not only accepting, but celebrating who you are. Try to be less critical of yourself. Even the most celebrated person in the world – the biggest film star, the biggest sex symbol – can have poor self-esteem from time to time. The Mountain meditation and self-acceptance meditations will help you to boost your self-esteem as you begin to accept yourself as you are. The meditation is available to download via rebrand.ly/resilientteen and read within the 'Meditations' section from page 115 to 146.

Chapter 5

Sitting with your pain

Wednesday 7th May, 1997 – Been tired. AAAAHHH! I'm so tired all the time. But I was thinking, maybe people are as tired as me but they're just stronger than me and have the willpower to keep going. But there could be those who would pass out if they were walking around in school after the lack of sleep I've had.

Wednesday 14th May, 1997 – I am getting so fed up with my lack of sleep that dad is going to take me to the doctors soon.

Monday 19th May 1997 – I'm exhausted. I have tried doing so much stuff to stop my lack of sleep but nothing seems to work. I have a blood test on Weds.

Wednesday 21st May, 1997 – I fainted after the blood test. He asked me whether I would or not and I said no because I haven't before! It was a horrible feeling. I am soooo weak.

Sometimes our bodies are crying out to us to tell us to stop and look after ourselves better. We can shoulder all sorts of pain but carry on in the hope that our bodies will just release it somehow without having to stop and fully acknowledge what is going on. The pain can come from all sorts of situations in our lives, the loss of a loved one, parents breaking up, a tragedy, a broken heart. Or perhaps the pain is something more undefinable, where we can't pin down why we feel such despair.

That pain isn't going to leave until you truly address it. Address it in a safe place, where you know you won't be interrupted. A place where you can air everything. This place is within you, if you give yourself the time. Have you given yourself the time to truly digest what is going on? Or have you stayed on the treadmill, too scared to stop and feel reality?

Perhaps fear is holding you back. Be brave and take the plunge, dig deep into your heart, the truth is tied up in knots. Unravel it all. Acknowledge it, sit with it, accept it. It will teach you more than you realise about yourself. You will feel strong again, you just need to spend a bit of time with yourself first. And more than this, you'll gain the wisdom to realise that this too will pass if you sit with it for long enough.

Mindful self-compassion

Without self-compassion, you may find that mindfulness unearths all sorts of feelings that otherwise remain sitting on your shoulders. You have heightened your awareness of those feelings, but with no healthy way to handle them you carry the weight with you wherever you go. Mindful self-compassion helps you to handle these uncomfortable feelings as they pop up in your mindfulness practice. It allows you to hold those feelings in a container of compassion much like you would care for your pet if he was sick. You would be there for your pet for as long as was needed, soothing him until he started to feel better. Mindful self-compassion can also be compared to how a good friend or family member truly listens to you when you are suffering. That person will stay with you, perhaps giving you a hug or holding your hand until the tears run dry.

I'm asking you, therefore, to consider being there for yourself. With mindful self-compassion YOU can be that person. YOU can be there for yourself. YOU can hold yourself in a container of compassion. Be kinder and more compassionate with yourself. Turn inwards and start listening to yourself, to how you truly feel about life. It may sound daunting, but it is the start of freedom…of releasing all that suppressed pain that you may have buried deep. The process may be painful, particularly if you have swallowed feelings for a long time and they're finally unearthing themselves. Those feelings may be strong and overwhelming. Perhaps that inner child that you ignored is starting to be heard and she is angry with you for bottling her up for all these years. Or perhaps she just wants to cry and cry and cry. The reality is that we can all carry a lot of pain within us and often we're surprised at how much we have stored up as we start to turn on the tap.

I'm not suggesting that you will feel better overnight. After all, this is not a quick fix. The healing process requires patience. Be kind to yourself if you're working through something. This is about welcoming the pain, embracing it, allowing it to be as it truly is. This is the opposite of bottling up or suppressing what is going on. You're not resisting the discomfort as it arises, instead you're allowing it to surface for as long as it wants. Use your breath to handle the discomfort and pain. As another squeeze, tightening or ache comes, tune into your breathing wherever you feel it most naturally. Pay attention to each in breath and out breath to ground you as you ride each wave of pain, one after the other. This will help you to welcome what surfaces, without the temptation to swallow your emotions. Let it all out, one tear at a time. If you don't let it all out you may find that your emotions resurface later in life, perhaps in the form of anger. It is healthy to release all of your emotions in a safe space using mindfulness techniques.

You may feel drained for a few days after releasing some pain, so choose to give yourself a break. Perhaps if you decide to start unearthing some truly painful, buried emotions, start on a Friday evening to give yourself the weekend to cradle your inner child, holding her in a container of compassion. That way, you are less likely to have to swallow it all again without fully addressing it. Perhaps you could do something comforting at the weekend to soothe you…Maybe take a nice, warm bath? Listen to some music? Go for a run or walk the dog? Choose something that soothes you in a healthy way while allowing you to be with your emotions for a bit longer.

Just as important as your physical space is creating enough emotional space for a self-compassion meditation. Allow enough time after the meditation to be with your pain for a while without having to immediately put on a brave face for others. The meditation is available to download via rebrand.ly/resilientteen and read within the 'Meditations' section from page 115 to 146. If you don't have time for the full meditation, but need to self-soothe, turn to Chapter 6 for a short meditation known as the 3-step breathing space.

Sometimes we need to open up through therapy or with the help of a close family member or friend. You may find that sharing your experiences with others will help you along the way. I recommend that if you decide to share your experience with another person ensure that whoever you confide in has the ability to listen to you with empathy and compassion, so that your healing process doesn't get disrupted. Check out Chapter 13 for a greater understanding of mindful listening.

Part 2

Chapter 6

Handling life's pressures

Now that the whys and wherefores of mindfulness have been explained and the longer, resilience-building, daily-practice mindfulness meditations have been explained, it is time to explore how you can use mindfulness to deal with specific instances in your life. In other words, mindfulness techniques that can be used on the spot, when you are faced with a sudden stressful situation (perhaps an incident of bullying, bad news, or you're overwhelmed by revision) or as you prepare to launch yourself into a stressful situation (such as a presentation or exam, or asking someone out on a date).

The short techniques in these chapters will help you in public situations. You may have concerns that you will look like a fool, with thoughts such as '*Will everyone laugh at me if I start closing my eyes and breathing funny?*' I want to reassure you that this can be something very private – no-one else even needs to know that you are focusing on your breathing. You are doing it internally, slowing down, pausing. And the more you practice, the more it will come to feel like a normal and natural part of the way you deal with challenges.

S.T.O.P.

The STOP technique is a particularly useful coping strategy to help you to handle stress and/or anxiety in the moment. This could be if you start to feel overwhelmed while revising, or you're about to ask someone out on a date, or you're about to play a football match, or about to read/sing at a family wedding, go for an interview for a summer job, etc. All those situations in life that make your legs turn to jelly.

The STOP technique is quick and easy to practice. It only requires 4 simple steps…

S – Stop what you're currently doing

T – Take one or more abdominal breaths

O – Observe your thoughts, feelings and sensations in this moment

P – Proceed mindfully

The first step is to stop what you're doing. I mean stop everything that you're doing, and that includes putting your phone down.

Next, take one or more abdominal breaths, focusing on your breathing in the belly, tuning in to each in-breath and out-breath. Give yourself some time to tune in to a few breaths. This can make a huge difference.

Now it is time to observe all the thoughts, feelings and sensations that are popping up for you right here right now. No need to hold back. Let them all come to the surface, acknowledging each of them one by one. This could be *'I'm going to fail'* or *'He will say no'* or *'I will screw this up'*. Remember that you're making up stories right now because you're stressed.

Finally, when you have fully acknowledged everything you're experiencing and you feel a bit more grounded, you can proceed mindfully (carrying on your day with renewed balance).

Exams

The STOP technique is particularly useful during exam season. When it comes to revision, you can try the technique before you start a piece of work. I remember when I revised, I wanting to store every single fact I could get my hands on. That wasn't helpful as I wasn't being selective and, instead, I was just acting on fear. I would rush through my revision in some sort of mild panic, trying to remember fact after fact after fact. The STOP technique can help to anchor you in the present moment, using your breathing so that you don't end up rushing through your revision. It can keep you focussed on the project rather than darting from one thing to another or checking your phone every two seconds to find out what everyone else is revising.

The STOP technique can also help you to prepare before an exam, to ground yourself in the body before your head starts racing too far ahead into the future. I recall anxiety kicking in as I started to make up stories about what would and wouldn't be in the test. When I had exams, I felt the need to rush everything and blurt out all I knew without necessarily answering the question that was being asked. Pausing before you start writing can really help you to gather yourself. Then, read the question again before planning your answer.

Grounding

Another exercise to try is the grounding exercise. Imagine you are in an exam situation, sitting at your desk just before the test papers are handed out. Your heart is pounding, you start nervously fidgeting with your pen and pencils, you take side glances at others to see what they're up to. Fear has hijacked you. Why not take those few minutes to use the following exercise to ground yourself when you most need it?

Tune into your breathing and ground yourself in the body. Let your attention drop to wherever you feel the breath most naturally (tummy/chest/nostrils). Notice the physical sensations of the breath, grounding you in the present. Fully experience each in-breath and each out-breath as you centre yourself.

Then take your attention to your feet. Place all of your attention there as you feel all four corners of your feet pressed into the ground. Notice how it feels to be supported by the ground. Remind yourself that you've got this. You're rooted and ready. Breathe and believe in this moment.

A few extra tips to handle stress during the exam period

- If it feels like your shoulders are up around your ears remember to keep an eye on your posture and have a stretch every now and then.

- If you find noise around you particularly distracting before an exam, consider going to the toilet or find a quiet space to steady yourself.

- Before the exam, try to avoid listening to others who could put you off. At that point it is too late to change what you have revised. You also don't want to pick up on their nerves. Remain grounded.

- How about treating yourself to, or making, pens or pencils with positive affirmations on? These little reminders can help in the midst of exam nerves.

- Stay present. You have this moment. Remember 'what ifs' are future thinking.

- See the exam as a chance to show off what you have learnt – see it as a positive rather than a negative.

Approaching a teacher when you're nervous

The grounding exercise and STOP technique are also useful if you need to speak to a teacher about something that makes you feel nervous. Perhaps you need to ask for some feedback on a piece of work that didn't achieve the grade you had hoped for, or you need to ask for an extension on a piece of work because chaos at home has affected your productivity. Whatever the reason, from time to time you will have to find the courage to speak to a teacher. Some teachers will be easy to speak to. Some will have a good rapport with you. However, talking to some teachers may be trickier. As in life, from time to time we all have to speak to people we struggle to bond with.

Try using the grounding technique or STOP technique before you approach a teacher to help you to remain calm and focussed. If the conversation becomes tricky or uncomfortable you can always try tuning into your breathing to remain centred and reduce the chances of reacting to the situation. Remember the fight or flight stress reaction within you – you may naturally veer towards a need to flee a scenario as soon as it feels challenging or you may veer towards a need to fight by arguing, disagreeing, resenting (or perhaps all three at once). Either way, you will benefit from a coping strategy that helps you to handle stress in these times, to keep those feet rooted to the floor and your mind focussed on the goal in hand. So, remember to tune into your breathing in these moments. Tune into the feeling of each in-breath and out-breath in your nostrils, chest or tummy. Then blow out the tension on the out breath. You may also find Chapter 9, on the subject of anger, useful if you struggle to remain calm when speaking to your teachers or to other adults or authority figures.

Receiving feedback from a teacher

As I mentioned in Chapter 2, our brains are prone to negativity bias, so when we receive feedback, we tend to remember one negative comment rather than a whole lot of positive comments. So, the next time you receive feedback from a teacher, how about using mindfulness to build more positive neural pathways in the brain? How can you do this? By remaining grounded during the feedback. Tune into your breathing, using the grounding technique or the STOP technique to help you focus on the information the teacher is giving you. If you remain calm, you are more likely to pick up on the positive points as well as the negative points. As you listen with a more balanced frame of mind you can store news as a neutral pathway or a positive pathway in the brain rather than as a purely negative pathway, as you may have done in the past.

The 3-step breathing space

This practice can help you to handle disappointment or sadness in the moment. Perhaps you feel hurt because someone has turned you down after you asked them out. Perhaps you're devastated because you've been dumped. Perhaps you're gutted because someone else got the job you really wanted. Take yourself somewhere for a few minutes where you can sit and practice this meditation to help with your emotions.

Start by getting comfortable in an upright position with your feet flat on the floor and shoulders nice and relaxed.

First step – Pay attention to what is happening in your body – all thoughts, feelings and sensations. Perhaps your stomach is lurching, your chest feels tight, or your shoulders are tense. Be open to whatever arises, not judging or trying to change anything, just acknowledging it all. Listen attentively to your body in this moment.

Second step – Let your attention drop into wherever you feel the breath most naturally. This could be in the tummy as it rises and falls with each in-breath and out-breath, the chest as the ribcage expands and contracts, or the nostrils. Tune into the physical sensations of the breath, grounding yourself in the present moment. Fully experience each in-breath and each out-breath as you centre yourself.

Third step – Expand awareness back to perceiving the body as a whole. Approach all discomfort, pain and tension with kindness and patience. You may find that your tummy is squeezing, your shoulders may be tense, your heart may be beating faster than normal. Use the breath to support you by breathing into these body sensations and feelings as they arise. Say to yourself, *'It is ok to feel like this'*. Breathe and say to yourself, *'Whatever has happened is already here. Let me feel it as best as I can'*. Say this to yourself as many times as you need to self-soothe. Welcoming the discomfort or pain helps to release it fully. If you still feel a bit low, how about saying to yourself *'I am enough just as I am'*. Say this to yourself as many times as you need, to provide comfort and reassurance.

By allowing your feelings and thoughts to surface you are accepting your situation as it truly is. This can help you to go about your day without carrying such a heavy burden on your shoulders. It doesn't mean that you will have removed the emotional pain from your body entirely, but it can help you to keep going.

When you are ready, place your hands over your face and gently wipe those tears, have a stretch, then go about your day with renewed strength and balance.

Giving a presentation

Ugh. The number of times I have built up anxiety about an upcoming presentation. All that preparation beforehand and yet you don't know how it is going to pan out when you're up there in front of everyone. The fear of forgetting everything is huge. The last thing you want is to stand there lost for words with everyone's eyes on you.

There is nothing wrong with being nervous. It means you care. There is a fine line between excitement and fear. So, you can choose to have fun. The next time you have an upcoming presentation, try using the techniques I have outlined in this chapter – the grounding technique, abdominal breathing and the STOP technique. Any one of these can help to ignite the 'rest and digest' system that turns your stress response down. Then, when you are grounded, you can choose to have fun. Try seeing it as an opportunity to show your peers and teacher what you know rather than viewing it as a nightmare scenario.

Another little tip is to practice the superhero pose shortly before you start your presentation. Research has proven[13] that this pose boosts confidence in only two minutes by increasing testosterone levels, which increase confidence. How about trying it now? You simply need to stand with your legs spread apart, hands on your hips and elbows bent. Now you feel a little bit more like a superhero.

---

13   Robin S. Posenberg Ph.D., 2011, 'Why you may want to stand like a superhero', https://www.psychologytoday.com/gb/blog/the-superheroes/201107/why-you-may-want-stand-superhero

Chapter 7

Bullying

Thursday 12th June 1997 – Not a nice day. Tamsin and others said I was square! I don't think she was joking so I cried to mum. Exam pressure is heating up, had a bath. Revised a tad.

Those dark, restless nights. Alone in my bed with my thoughts. My mind spinning. A sense of dread creeping over my body. The questions, oh so many questions... 'Will they talk to me tomorrow? Will they say I'm square again? Will they call me something else? Will I be able to handle it?' And the biggest question that swirled around in my brain over and over again: 'Why me??? Why...me???? Was I too friendly? Did I smile too much? Did I say the wrong thing at lunch? Did I say the wrong thing at PE? Did I laugh too much at their jokes? Or not enough at their jokes? Was I too silly in history?'

So many reasons would pop into my head, endless stories that I made up to try to understand why it started in the first place. I assumed I had done something to cause them to be so mean.

I tried EVERYTHING to get them to like me. I sang along to their Radiohead songs in the tuck shop queue. To which Tamsin said, *"I didn't think you would know a song like that"*, as if I had been hidden away in a box, removed from life and not allowed to listen to a radio. I knew most of the lyrics, but that wasn't enough. I thought perhaps I wasn't seen as cool enough. Surely singing along to a song they liked would show them that I was. I desperately wanted to be included, to be liked. Not singled out, picked on relentlessly. And it was relentless.

A lot of what happened went unnoticed by the other girls at school. Or that is how it seemed. Looking back, I imagine some noticed but didn't say anything. Perhaps they were afraid that if they said something, they would get picked on too. Or perhaps their popularity would have plummeted if they spoke up for me. So, no-one said anything.

Bullying is rife

Everyone's experience of bullying is different. It can take different forms, sometimes it may just come across as 'banter' to others yet it causes so much pain to the person who is experiencing it. It may be physical, or verbal, or psychological in form. It can be very snide and secretive, or very open and public. It can be really hard when others are singing the praises of a bully who is outwardly friendly and charming yet secretly nasty to you. Bullying takes lots of shapes and sizes and everyone's personal experience of bullying is valid. You can be bullied for all sorts of reasons – your sexuality, your gender, your intelligence, your looks, your personality, your religious preferences, your race, and the list goes on.

According to the Annual Bullying Survey by Ditch the Label,[14] 1 out of 5 young people has been victimised by bullying. Furthermore, almost 1 in 2 of those victimised feel depressed and 1 in 3 have suicidal thoughts. Those are shocking and heart-breaking statistics. If you think about it, if you're lucky enough to not be targeted by bullies, it is highly likely that one of your close friends is not so lucky.

I was fortunate that social media didn't exist when I was a teen, as that may have escalated the classroom bullying that I experienced. Even on the toughest days, I knew that I would have a break from it all when I got home. With mobile phones attached to our palms these days, anyone experiencing bullying may feel that there is no escape. Now it feels as if, via social media, bullies can enter your home life too. This is where addiction to mobile phones really takes its toll. As teenagers, FOMO has you locked in this need to be constantly con-

---

[14] Dr. Liam Hackett, CEO of Ditch the Label, 2019, The Annual Bullying Survey 2019, https://www.ditchthelabel.org/research-papers/the-annual-bullying-survey-2019/ p6.

nected, to sleep with your phone as close to you as possible. You may even sleep with your phone under your pillow! If this is the case and you're being bullied, I can't begin to imagine the level of emotional pain you experience before you go to sleep. If the last thing you see before you attempt to drop off to sleep is a hurtful comment aimed at you, it is highly likely to affect your self-esteem and self-acceptance. I advise you to have a good think about your relationship with your phone and with social media in particular. In Chapter 11 we'll explore the mindful use of social media.

How can mindfulness help you if you're being bullied?

Often bullies are looking for a reaction, they want to know they have affected you in some way. Oh, the number of times I would lie awake at night trying to prepare the perfect comeback to their cruel jibes! But it wasn't in my nature to be harsh. Instead, when they started picking on me, I went quiet, attempting to somehow hide away and not be spotted. This didn't work, as they could see from my face that I had been crying, they knew they were getting to me. Some people may choose to explode at their bullies, shouting back with nasty comments. This can also fuel the fire because the bullies can see that their bullying has caused a reaction. They want you to react with an emotional outburst of some sort to show that they have got to you, rather than a calm response that gives the impression that their comments mean nothing.

How can mindfulness help you in this scenario? Unfortunately, mindfulness can't magically make the bully see the light and stop their abuse. But it can help you to handle the onslaught by boosting your resilience. Remember the quote from the Blurt Foundation… *"Resilience is about getting through, and dealing with, the negative events, and then picking yourself up afterwards…"*

Learning to surf life's waves one by one. And the bullying wave is a big one. I highly recommend meditating in the morning to boost your resilience for the day ahead. The mountain meditation is particularly beneficial when it comes to bullying. It can empower you with confidence and emotional balance, regardless of what is going on around you. How about practicing it in the morning before you go to school, or before you go out anywhere that you are likely to encounter the bullies. The solid, unwavering mass of a mountain remains unmoved regardless of the weather and seasonal patterns circling around it. It remains its essential self at all times. You can take inspiration from the mountain. You can remain unmoved by what is going on around you. The voices that threaten to push you over can be seen as merely voices in the rain and wind. They will pass by, just as the weather and seasons pass over the mountain. Those voices don't reflect who you are. You have your own unique experiences and views of the world. You won't let those icy winds push you over or make you question yourself. You are enough. You are worthy of love and acceptance. Your self-esteem doesn't depend on what others think of you. You blow out the tension in meditations, blow out those chilly winds that try to diminish you. You are capable of so much. You won't let those winds hold you back from your essential self. You remain unmoved by the weather. Solid and strong in the face of whatever comes your way. You validate yourself and yourself is enough. See 'Meditations' from page 115 to 146 for the written version.

Mindfulness and resilience in the face of a bully attack

It is important to understand that in any situation, you have a choice whether to **respond** or **react**. When we react, it is often sudden, emotional and not thought through. Bullies thrive on getting a reaction from their victims, so I advise you to consider responding instead. A response involves pausing, taking a breath, then approaching the situation calmly. When you pause, you turn down your fight/flight reaction and instead ignite the parasympathetic nervous system (rest and digest system) which signals to the body that everything is ok. It turns down the stress response and allows information to flow more easily to the prefrontal cortex, the decision-making part of the brain. This allows you to respond rationally rather than react emotionally. It helps you to cope with the discomfort and pain you are experiencing and allows for a more measured and centred response to surface.

In order to remain centred during a bully attack, try tuning into your breathing and ground yourself in the body with the following exercise…

Let your attention drop into wherever you feel the breath most naturally in your body (this could be your tummy, your chest or your nostrils). Notice the physical sensations of each in-breath and out-breath as you ground yourself in the present moment. Keep focussing on this as the voices around you try to throw you off balance.

Then take your attention to your feet. Place all of your attention there as you feel all four corners of your feet pressed into the ground. Notice how it feels to be supported by the ground. Remember that you can remain rooted in the face of any onslaught coming your way.

Remind yourself that you've got this, you can handle this moment, and the next, and the next…

Try not to be put off by worries about the bullies noticing what you're up to. Remember that this grounding tool is an internal experience. It is only something that you know about so the bullies won't be able to pick on you about it. As I've said in the introduction, practising mindfulness is like having a hidden superpower. It can keep us strong in the face of any onslaught.

What can you do after the attack has finished?

Unfortunately, it is unlikely that you'll be able to go straight home and hide in your bed, crying into your pillow. You will probably have to continue going about your day. You need to find a way to gather yourself quickly. You may find a short meditation helpful to give you a little space to digest what has happened. The 3-step breathing space (see page 63) only takes a few minutes and can help to soothe you. It can be practised somewhere safe in school during a break (in some cases that may have to be the school toilet – trust me it's worth a shot).

By allowing your feelings and thoughts to surface, you are accepting your situation as it truly is. This can help you to go about your day without carrying such a heavy burden on your shoulders. It doesn't mean that you have removed the pain from your body entirely, but it can help you to keep going after a bullying attack.

It may seem a bit alien to you to comfort yourself in this way, but imagine if you were with a friend who was struggling. You would repeat words of comfort until your friend felt better. By accepting your true emotions and thoughts, you are helping yourself to feel better, so that you can respond more skilfully to a negative situation. This allows you to cope with the stress of bullying in a healthier way.

Healthily releasing emotions when you get home

It is important to understand that you didn't cause this. When we're bullied, we can easily get caught up in self-attack mode. We assume that we did something to cause others to be so mean. Almost as if we deserve the pain. This is absolutely not the case. No-one deserves to be bullied. This is merely another made-up story in your head to try to handle the suffering you're going through. You can so easily get stuck making up story after story to explain why you're treated poorly, to try to understand the root cause of your suffering. Trust me, you have done nothing wrong. You didn't cause this storm. What you need to do is look after yourself as you surf those bully waves.

The self-compassion meditation can help you to do this, see 'Meditations' from page 115 to 146. Breathing techniques can help you to keep going at school in the middle of the attack, but it is really important that you release the emotional pain when you get home. You can take down that brave face, that mask you've been wearing to get through your day. Now you can let it all out in your safe place.

The self-acceptance meditation is also really useful for bullying, see 'Meditations' from page 115 to 146. It reminds you to be kind to yourself and accept yourself as you are rather than believing the vicious words that the bullies are saying. Continue practicing it to it to keep love in your heart.

Have patience

Know this: things will change. Right now, you may feel like nothing will change, that the bullies will bully you forever. But nothing is permanent. Just as we're confident that the seasons and the weather will change, life as you know it right now will also change.

Life is one big rollercoaster of ups and downs. You may find that some days are easier than others. The bullies may not speak to you some days, maybe they'll target someone else or they're off sick. Or perhaps they're feeling less bully-like today. Try not to cling to those easier days or get dragged down too much by the tougher days. Take every day as it comes, but walk into school with the tools you're learning in this book. Remember the words of Jon Kabat Zinn, *"You can't stop the waves but you can learn to surf"*.[15]

Marshmallows in my hair

I went to a sleepover once and fell asleep earlier than everyone else. When I woke up, I had a mask on my face and marshmallows stuck in my hair. I asked my friend what happened and she told me that some of the girls, including her, decided to put marshmallows in my hair while I slept. She felt guilty about it but, apparently, it was Hazel's idea. Hazel was friends with Tamsin and Lydia, they often all hung out together (and bullied people as a group). I got up and tried to wash the sticky marshmallows out of my hair, trying not to cry. My friend helped me, which was kind of her. With the exception of Hazel, all those girls behaved out of character that night. They wouldn't normally choose to do something that could upset someone else like that. I was hurt. Their actions were influenced by someone else. Perhaps each girl thought *'If I go along with the crowd then I'm not the target, someone else is'*. Or perhaps they didn't think their actions through. They went against their true nature because of their need to be validated by someone else.

> **"Wrong is wrong, even if everyone is doing it. Right is right, even if no-one is doing it."**
>
> **Buddha**

So, remember to remain true to yourself. Your brain is geared towards being part of the group, so there will be times when you bend to please others. But you need to be alert to the possibility of being taken advantage of to the point where you don't recognise yourself, perhaps even to the point of joining in with the bullying of others. Believe me, doing something that goes against your nature can make you feel a whole lot worse. If you are normally a kind person, then even a sniff of nastiness

---

15 Jon-Kabat-Zinn, Ph.D. 2004, *Wherever You Go, There You Are: Mindfulness Meditation for Everyday Life*, Piatkus, p30.

can cause such hideous guilt and shame inside of you that it really isn't worth it. So, be mindful of your actions. Your conscience won't let you rest anyway. Even if you do something that hurts someone else for external validation, your conscience won't let it go. And your conscience is persistent.

As a fully grown adult and mindfulness coach, I am learning to see the bigger picture more often. To understand that people act in unkind ways due to deep rooted issues. Something may be going on at home that is causing their behaviour. It doesn't come out of nowhere. For any bullies reading this, I imagine it may be hard to admit what you're doing. You may downplay your actions as mere 'banter', shoving aside the thought that you may actually be harming someone with your words. Or you may intentionally want to hurt someone with a vicious tongue or attitude. Could this be a release of your own frustrations in life? For you I have written a letter. This letter is written from a more mindful place with an intention to show empathy and guidance on how to change, if you want to.

Dear Bully

No child is born a bully. You must be experiencing some pretty painful stuff in your life to act the way you do at school. I'm sorry for the pain you're experiencing. I am not pointing the finger, as blame gets us nowhere. Often bullies are bullied themselves beneath the surface. Are you bullied by someone at home? Perhaps you are bullying yourself owing to some form of unmet need? Perhaps you find that releasing your frustration onto others is the easiest thing to do in your circumstances. Perhaps you feel it is the only way to survive each day.

Let me tell you…pain just leads to more pain. Trampling on others is not going to help. The pain you unleash onto others becomes pain for them. If you think this is the way to boost your self-esteem, you are wrong. It may get you some temporary attention from others at school but it won't give you the acceptance and love you secretly crave. That acceptance and love needs to start with you. You need to hold yourself accountable. You need to look after yourself better. Be brave and learn a new healthy way to release your pain. You, more than anyone, would benefit from self-compassion.

Ask yourself…how is your conscience? Do you sleep well at night? Which of your needs are unmet? Acknowledge them. Sit with the pain in all its hard-edged wisdom. It will teach you more about yourself than you realise. You will feel strong again, you just need to spend a bit of time with yourself first. And, if you sit with it for long enough, you'll gain the wisdom to realise that this too shall pass.

So, open up and take down that armour. It doesn't have to be a fight. You don't have to be that person. You can raise yourself up. You have permission to change, for every day is a new start. A new beginning. A new opportunity to become a stronger, kinder person. You can make the change. The more you work on yourself, the more you may realise the hurt you have inflicted on others. Forgive yourself for this. You are only human after all and we all make mistakes. You may even decide to apologise one day. This is all possible once you start to truly listen to yourself. We all have a past, but we don't have to let it define us. We can say 'Yes, I did that. Yes, I said those things. And I learnt from them. And I grew. And now I am so much more than that helpless kid. I am strong. I am brave. I am love and I will treat every person I meet with the love I was lacking before.'

Best wishes

Nicola

Everyone's experience of bullying is different. It takes many forms and hurts in many ways. Use mindfulness techniques to help you to handle the enormity of emotions that can come with bullying. The mountain meditation will help to keep you grounded in preparation for your day ahead and breathing techniques will help you to handle a bully attack in the moment. The mindful self-compassion meditation and self-acceptance meditation will help you to release the build-up of emotions when you get home and remind you to be kind to yourself. As for those of you who are currently bullying others, try some mindful self-compassion or self-acceptance to release your built-up emotions. We can all grow as people and show more empathy towards others. Every day is a new day where we can choose to be gentler with each other's hearts.

Chapter 8

When life at home is turned upside down

Thursday 24th July 1997 – I'm crying. I've just realised that mum and dad are getting a DIVORCE. I had known earlier but never really took it in. Told Melz how I felt on the phone today.

Sometimes the people with the biggest smiles hold the most pain. There is pain behind your eyes. There is pain in your heart. You're walking around wearing a mask. It's a good mask. It helps you to get through every day. But it's a mask nonetheless. It isn't the real you. You smile at your friends on the way to school. You laugh at the joke that boy keeps repeating to everyone he sees. You hold your head up, you pull your shoulders back, you keep going. But inside, there is turmoil. There is pain.

If you are constantly putting on a brave face when tensions are high at home, know that you're not alone. Tension appears in every house, we're all just masters at hiding it from the outside world.

Perhaps something big has happened, such as a family member becoming unwell, your parents announcing their divorce, or your family suddenly facing significant financial troubles. Whatever may be going on at home, when things are unsettled it can feel like a dark cloud is constantly above you.

If your parents are struggling with a heavy weight on their shoulders, you may struggle to open up to them fully. Perhaps they check in with you to see if you're ok, but you don't want to burden them with more stress. You could end up feeling very alone, feeling like there is no room for you emotionally. No room for you to offload.

Or what if you've opened up to your parents about something private that you've been grappling with for ages, and you've been met with anger or disappointment? What if you've been going through some changes internally or figured out who you really are or want to be, you've finally had the courage to divulge and you've been met with disapproval? It could be anything from your gender identity or sexuality to veganism or your religious beliefs. Perhaps your parents are angry or disapproving about your choices or perhaps they are fighting with each other over it. Whatever may be happening, the tension in your house is palpable. How can you build resilience in a house full of tension?

Mindful self-compassion is a good starting point. You can soothe yourself, meet your pain with tenderness. Look after yourself while life around you crumbles. For your life will change again and your world will be put back together again piece by piece. It may take some time for your support network to be up and running fully so, in the meantime, take care of yourself.

I get it. You weren't prepared for this pain. You can prepare for an exam, you can know every single line of your upcoming play, you can have the perfect outfit for that gig you're going to at the weekend, but you can never prepare for the day that your home life is turned upside down.

I remember consoling a friend when I was younger. She had recently found out her parents were splitting up. We were at a club one night when I realised she had not come back from the toilets for a while. I found her crying in a cubicle. I sat outside listening to her sobs. I told her *"I know it feels like this situation won't go away but, trust me, it will get easier. Your parents will feel better and you will feel better. Do you want this situation to hold you back from succeeding in your life or do you want to take this pain and channel it into propelling you forward? You can do it all. You can carry on. You can be everything you want to be."* Her pain didn't go away that night, but she started to see that things would get better, that life would change. Undoubtedly, she experienced more nights like that – nights of pain and heartache. Nights when she allowed the pain to come to the surface, sat with it, acknowledged and released it in a healthy way.

You may find that your sleep is affected during particularly difficult times. Perhaps you feel there is too much pain in your heart to allow you to settle down at night or too much agitation in the air to allow you to relax. The tension may build around you. You need to release that tension, but you don't know how.

Who can you turn to in the middle of the storm? Yourself.

Who will help you with your pain? Yourself.

Who will be there for you time and time again? Yourself.

Turn towards yourself for strength. Turn towards yourself for love. Turn towards yourself for kindness. It is all there for the taking.

YOU can be the one to steady yourself in the eye of the storm. YOU can handle this pain, and the next batch of pain that may be coming, and the pain after that.

It is about acknowledging the pain in all its beautiful glory. Facing it head on and saying, this REALLY hurts. No seriously, this hurts in ways that can't be explained. Labelling it for what it is. Saying it over and over to yourself until it is fully acknowledged, known for what it truly is. Then comes acceptance. But the first step in healing is to acknowledge the pain in the first place.

Confide in yourself. Don't shy away from the tough bits. Perhaps what's going on inside is that you're angry at your dad for getting cancer; perhaps you're confused and hurt because your parents are breaking up; perhaps you want to side with your brother who is always fighting with your parents. Perhaps you feel guilty for wanting to run a million miles away from it all. When things are tense at home it can spark all sorts of confusing emotions within you. How can I be angry at dad for getting cancer, but I am? How can I live in two homes? Of course, my brother's a (insert swear word here), but I still wish mum and dad wouldn't be so hard on him? It's all muddy. Look inside yourself and start releasing that clogged up, muddy, confused interior. Trust me, if you don't start letting it out it could come back to haunt you years from now.

Whatever you're going through in life right now, I highly recommend the mindful self-compassion meditation to help you to handle your pain. This meditation will allow you to start sitting with your pain rather than trying to bury it deep, or avoiding it with distraction. Go deep, get to the root of your suffering, your inner child needs it. Why not give the self-compassion meditation a go right now? If you haven't already tried it, or need to reacquaint yourself with it, see 'Meditations' from page 115 to 146. And remember to self soothe too. Simply placing a hand on your heart can provide comfort during particularly rocky times.

I also need to acknowledge that some of you may be experiencing ongoing tension in the house where there appears to be no end in sight – an alcoholic or otherwise addicted parent or sibling, a family member with ongoing disruptive mental health problems, a violent parent or sibling, to name but a few examples. If this is the case, whilst mindful self-compassion may help, I also recommend that you seek external support from a trusted source.[16]

Creating quiet head space

Sometimes you may not feel like digging deep into your emotions using a mindful self-compassion meditation but you still may require some quiet head space away from the noise around you. After all, regardless of what is going on at home, we still have certain life requirements that can't wait. You may find that you have an upcoming exam that you need to prepare for or another piece of work that can't wait. You need some quiet head space amongst the noise of arguing parents or crying siblings. I recommend finding a pair of headphones and choosing to meditate for a bit. It doesn't have to be a long time, just enough to ground you before you start a piece of work.

The Breathing Meditation is a great meditation for grounding you in the moment and releasing tension in the body. Sit on a chair in an upright position or on the floor in a cross-legged position and connect with your breathing while repeating phrases to release tension in the body. The key phrase I use in this meditation is from Thich Nhat Hanh who says *"Breathing in I'm aware of my body, breathing out I celebrate my body. Breathing in, I feel calm in my body. Breathing out I release the tension*

---

[16] There are specific charities out there to help young people such as Young Minds, Childline, Children of Addicted Parents and People (COAP), The National Association for Children of Alcoholics (NOACA)…check out princes-trust.org.uk for a full list.

in my body…"[17] Why not try the meditation the next time your house is overcome with noisy disruption? If you have more time, I recommend practicing the Body Scan which also helps to release tension in the body. Both the Breathing Meditation and the Body Scan meditation are available to download via rebrand.ly/resilientteen and within the 'Meditations' section from page 115 to 146.

Absorbing other people's pain

In his book *Anger: Buddhist Wisdom for Cooling the Flames*, Thich Nhat Hanh[18] talks about what can happen if you listen too much to other people's suffering and how it can affect your balance. There is a skill to listening well. He says, *"If you listen too much to the suffering, the anger of other people, you will be affected. You will be in touch only with suffering and you won't have the opportunity to be in touch with other positive elements. This will destroy your balance."*

He reminds us that the best way to heal is to find things that nourish us and nature is one of his many suggestions. I was very lucky to grow up on a farm, so I could turn to nature for nourishment whenever I needed it.

The soothing wisdom of nature

When I felt overwhelmed with emotions, I would step outside my door and go for a walk. Not too far, but far enough away from the house to stop in a field and breathe. I would take in the air, allowing it to fill my body. Wholesome fresh air that allowed me to just be. I didn't have to be anything else at that point. I could just be with the wind. I could feel it on my face, I could feel it blowing against my body. Almost trying to knock me over, almost imitating my life, as if to goad me with the question '*Can you handle this?*'

I would stop to look at a tree swaying in the breeze, seeing how it withstood the wind and rain. If a tree could withstand the challenges it faced, so could I. Every push and shove reminded me that I was strong and

---

17 Thich Nhat Hanh, posted 2018, 'Breathing In', https://thichnhathanh quotecollective.com/2018/07/17/breathing-in/

18 Thich Nhat Hanh, 2011, *Anger: Buddhist Wisdom for Cooling the Flames*, Random House audiobooks.

capable of withstanding any storm. I could be like a tree and stand tall, rooted in the face of pain. I looked up at the clouds and noticed how they were dark and stormy too, their heaviness mimicking how I felt. Heavy with pain that I didn't want to address. Full of feelings. Full of frustration. And yet peeking through the dark clouds was a little bit of sunshine. Not a lot. But a tiny ray of hope just peeking through as if to say hello. As if to say…you CAN get through this. You WILL get through this. Nature was soothing me. Soothing me and reassuring me. I know now from my research into mindfulness that we are all connected. This world is one. It helped me to breathe deeper as my anger gradually dissipated. A beam of sunshine was calling to me, reassuring me that it would be ok in the end.

So, the next time you feel overwhelmed with emotions, why not try calling on nature. Can you get outside? If you can't, how about opening your window? What sounds can you hear? Can you hear birds tweeting amidst all the other sounds around you? Can you feel a breeze on your face? Can you take a few mindful breaths to energise yourself with fresh air? It can help to blow away the tension. Breathing out that tension that builds up before it becomes too much and you end up exploding at someone in frustration. If you can get outside, can you feel the wind against your body? Is it blowing your hair? Is it strong enough to push against you? What can you see in front of you? A mass of blue sky? Or a dark and stormy sky? What are the clouds doing? Are they moving fast or slow? If they're moving fast, perhaps they're racing along like your mind, or perhaps they're slower. Can you tune into that, steadying your mind by breathing along to the pace of the clouds? Is there a tree you can look up at? Can you imagine how old that tree is and all the types of weather it has withstood over the years? Nature grounds us, it is wise, it shows us the bigger picture, if only we take a moment to tune into it.

Chapter 9

A healthy approach to managing anger

"Holding on to anger is like drinking poison and expecting the other person to die."

Buddha

Once, on a night out with a friend from my school days, I bumped into one of my old bullies from school. Seeing the person who had caused so much pain in my teens caused a strong reaction in my body. I felt those old familiar butterflies in my tummy. I was still carrying around my fear from the past. She came up to me and said hello, as if we had always been friends. I was polite. I smiled. I responded calmly, said hello back, and went along with the pretence that we were friends in order to keep the peace.

Later that night, I was in the toilet with my friend. The bully came in with her friend. She hugged my friend and started to chat to the two of us, as if nothing had happened at school. RAGE overwhelmed me. It came firing out of me like a cannon! I can't remember exactly what she said, but I responded by shouting at her *"Friend? You're not my friend! You treated me like **** at school!"*

She was very surprised, as she was unaware of my emotions, and unaware of the pain bubbling up inside me. She had expected predictable smiley Nicky. Instead, the rage came out in full force. Although she was surprised, she gave no clear acknowledgement. What did I want her to say? *"You're right. I was a complete ***** to you at school and I'm so sorry"*. But would that have been enough for me? Probably not. I was far too angry to be consoled. My belly was hot with emotion. Every part of my being wanted to slap her. That's the truth. I wanted to slap her. But I didn't. Instead I pushed her friend. Yes, I pushed her friend. Simply because she was trying to intervene. I turned to my friend then, hoping for support and proof, "*Didn't she? Didn't she bully me at school!*" But my friend didn't stand up for me. OH, THE RAGE. The rage was actually causing me pain. I was in pain not only because no-one would acknowledge what I had been through, but my friend wasn't backing me up.

A few days later I received an email from the girl who had bullied me, apologising for her behaviour at school. I appreciated that. It didn't remove the pain but it certainly helped to finally have it acknowledged.

If you don't fully listen to the emotional pain within you it will come out like a foghorn in later life. When I was a teen, I bottled up my pain for years, thinking that I could bury it so deep it would never surface again. I was wrong, it surfaced again in the form of anger. From weeping inner child to exploding ape. Oh, was I angry! I would feel the rage boiling up inside of me at the slightest trigger.

I can recall many incidents in my life when rage took over. Looking back, I believe a lot of that anger stemmed from suppressed emotions. Emotions that I didn't acknowledge, emotions that I didn't fully pay attention to, let alone accept. Emotions that I'd simply carried around with me. Certain situations in my present can still trigger these past emotions. However, these days, I can use mindfulness to handle them better. I notice more quickly how I feel and I can identify if the feeling is based on reality (the here and now) or based on some situation from the past. I can then use mindfulness tools and self-compassion tools to handle the emotion in an appropriate way.

Finding better ways to deal with anger

The first step to dealing with anger is to understand that feeling angry is perfectly normal. Anger is a natural human emotion. If someone mistreats you, you're likely to feel the flames of anger rising up inside. The struggle you face is how to deal with the anger in a healthy way, so that you look after yourself and those around you who may also be affected. Anger can often rear its ugly head when you feel that something is unjust –

the thought that one thing should have happened rather than another. Different things will trigger anger, depending on how you interpret the world around you.

Avoiding anger traps

Mindfulness can help to cool down anger.

Breathing techniques help us to handle it in the moment, grounding us in the here and now, and reducing our chances of a sudden reaction. Thich Nhat Hanh[19] writes, *"Breathing in, I feel my anger. Breathing out, I smile. I stay with my breathing, so I won't lose myself"*.

Connecting with our bodies more also helps to unearth how we truly feel about something by unravelling what is going on beneath the surface. We can identify the emotions that fuel our anger. Perhaps deep down you're feeling sad rather than angry. Perhaps you're igniting old frustrations from the past and they are stirring you up more than what is happening in the present.

Or perhaps you're caught up in negative thought patterns or **Mind Traps** that feed the anger. Thoughts patterns can trap us, encircling us in a vicious cycle of negative thinking where we're unable to see what is really going on, preventing us from popping our heads up, like meercats, to take a look around and see life as it truly is.

Here are some examples of the mind traps that we can get caught in…

Overgeneralising. This involves using words such as '*always*' or '*never*'. '*He always gets to…I never get to…*' These words can fuel your internal fire very quickly and create a sense of permanence. It's easy to get caught in a spiral of negativity when you assume that things will not change, and that life will remain the same forever.

Discounting the positive. When we use the word 'but', such as in "*I accept your apology **but** I'm still mad about it*", it discounts the positive and gives more weight to the negative. Try replacing 'but' with the more neutral word 'and'.

Catastrophising. In other words, making a mountain out of a mole hill. This often increases anxiety. For example, your sister borrows

---

[19] Thich Nhat Hanh, 2006, *Present Moment Wonderful Moment: Mindfulness Verses for Daily Living*, Parallax Press, p91.

your favourite jumper without asking and accidentally ruins it. The worry builds in your head to the point where you start creating stories and believing them, such as *"My sister destroyed my favourite jumper and I'll never be able to forgive her. I will never find another jumper as nice as that. She has ruined my life"*. We waste a lot of energy getting caught in up in our own disaster movies!

Mindreading. This is when you assume that you can read someone's mind and you presume they are thinking something negative about you. This can lead to anxiety and depression as you become convinced that others think the worst of you. I've been trapped in this one so many times! When I was bullied, I assumed that everyone disliked me and had unkind thoughts about me. When I was at work, I assumed that a raised eyebrow from my boss meant she thought I was useless at my job and was going to fire me (see catastrophizing, above!). All of these stories were in my head with no real facts to support them. The next time you get caught up in mindreading, take a few conscious breaths. Then, when you feel that your tension has lifted a little, ask yourself what the facts are. When you break your mindreading story down to rational facts you start to realise you were caught up in a trance and you can choose to shake off the trance and live in the present moment.

Using the word 'should'. Using the word 'should' can trigger feelings of resentment towards others. They should have done/said such and such and you're angry because they didn't do/say what you expected – like my friend who 'should have' stood up for me when I asked her to back up that I had been bullied at school. Try replacing the word with 'could' instead.

Blaming. This is where you don't take responsibility for your actions and, instead, point the finger elsewhere.

Inspirational thinker Dr Brene Brown, in her brilliant animated YouTube talk[20] on blame says,

"Blame is simply this discharging of discomfort and pain. Blaming is simply a way that we discharge anger. People who blame a lot seldom have the tenacity and grit to actually hold people accountable because we

---

20 Dr Brene Brown, 2015, 'Dr Brene Brown on Blame', https://www.youtube.com/watch?v=RZWf2_2L2v8

spend all of our energy raging for 15 seconds and figuring out whose fault something is. And blaming's very corrosive in relationships and its one of the reasons we miss our opportunities for empathy. Because when something happens and we're hearing a story, we're not really listening, we're making the connections as quickly as possible about whose fault something is."

Using mindfulness to dissolve anger

Mindfulness helps us to recognise and catch these negative thought patterns before they take hold of our bodies, trapping us in a spiral of negativity and anger. By practicing mindfulness on a regular basis, we can become aware of these mind traps and learn to pause and observe what is truly happening in daily life. This helps us to become more aware of what our minds are up to. As we become aware of these thought patterns, we can choose whether to believe them or not. Mindfulness helps us to **consciously respond rather than react**.

I have to find some way to release anger, otherwise it boils up inside and I explode in a rage. If that happens, I end up hurting my loved ones and causing further pain for everyone. Instead, I have to find a healthy outlet to release my anger. One way is by tuning into my breathing and using the following breathing exercise to healthily breathe out tension…

Mini breathing exercise for anger

Find a safe place where you can take a moment on your own to anchor yourself with your breathing. Speaking or acting when angry will only cause more suffering for you and those around you. In order to limit the potential damage, make the conscious decision to walk into a different space. This could be the bathroom, your bedroom, or perhaps the garden. I am not suggesting that you leave the house or wherever you happen to be, as this may not be safe, and your safety matters. Instead, choose somewhere safe where you can continue to look after yourself.

Start by paying attention to your breathing, noticing what is happening to your body on each in-breath and each out-breath. Do you feel it more in your tummy as it rises and falls? Do you feel it more in your chest as it expands and contracts? Do you feel it more in your nose as the breath flows through your nostrils?

Try to see the in-breath as an opportunity to take in more air or space and the out-breath as a release, letting go of any tension you're holding onto. Perhaps try using the words of Thich Nhat Hanh[21] *"Breathing in, I feel my anger. Breathing out, I smile. I stay with my breathing so I won't lose myself."* Repeat this over and over until you feel the fire in your belly start to cool down.

You may notice your shoulders start to drop or your jaw to unclench or your chest loosening. This may take a while, so be patient with yourself. Remember, the key is to not speak or act when angry, but rather to wait until the anger has completely passed through you.

As you start to calm down, you may become aware of hidden thoughts or feelings that fuelled your anger. You may even find that you have an unmet need buried deep in amongst the flames which is finally showing itself. This is the time for acknowledgement and acceptance. Give yourself the time to digest what is going on, acknowledging and accepting everything that comes up. Use the breath to support you as you allow all body sensations and feelings to arise. Say to yourself *'It is ok to feel like this.'* Say this to yourself as many times as required.

As you accept a thought, your body may unearth further feelings and sensations you may not have felt before. You may notice squeezing or knots in your stomach, tight shoulders, a clenched jaw, a faster heartbeat. Again, say to yourself *'It is ok to feel like this.'* Say this to yourself as many times as you need to provide comfort and reassurance.

By accepting your true emotions and thoughts you can respond more skilfully to a situation rather than reacting with negative emotions. You have intervened in the automatic stress response and cooled the flames of anger, allowing you to see things from a more measured perspective, thus helping you to respond rather than react.

Tuning into your senses

Another way to use mindfulness as a tool to reduce your anger is by tuning into your senses. Try paying attention to sounds around you, perhaps listening to music or opening a window so that you can hear

---

21 Thich Nhat Hanh, 2006, *Present Moment Wonderful Moment: Mindfulness Verses for Daily Living*, Parallax Press, p91.

the birds outside or a plane passing overhead. When you tune into your senses you are connecting with the present moment which takes you off the anger treadmill. If you truly connect with the present you will not be living in the past, replaying an argument in your head, or in the future, imaging a future conversation with the person for whom you feel the anger.

You can also tune into your senses in other ways. You could try slowly eating a comforting snack to use the sense of taste to soothe you. Or use your sense of sight by going for a walk and looking up at the trees or noticing the birds in the sky, or any other details that will calm you. Or find something around you, such as a blanket or a pet, the touch of which soothes you. Or take in the comforting smells around you of freshly cut grass, flowers on the table, a roast in the oven, or whatever else brings you comfort.

Mindful exercise

Another technique to cool down anger is to engage in mindful exercise. By this I mean paying attention to how your muscles feel as they tense and release during exercise. I find that when I run mindfully i.e. paying attention to how my thighs feel and connect with other body sensations as I run, I am tuning into the present moment. This helps me to notice if I'm replaying an argument in my head and allows me to release the tension healthily.

Your unmet emotional needs

Sometimes when you're angry it's because a certain emotional need hasn't been met. Occasionally, that unmet need becomes apparent while you're mid-argument with someone but perhaps you don't want to admit it. Or you may find that you have no idea why you feel the way you do…you just have lots of rage. If you struggle to understand your feelings or to connect with your body you may find the self-compassion meditation useful (see 'Meditations' from page 115 to 146). It is particularly beneficial for those who tend to deeply bury their emotions. A self-compassion meditation starts the process of being more compassionate towards yourself. It takes you off the self-judgement treadmill and allows you to get to know yourself better, helping you to understand why you feel the anger. By showing compassion towards yourself you let your guard down a little, taking down that armour and revealing who you truly are beneath the surface. The unmet need will show itself if you're ready to listen. Once you understand the unmet need, a self-compassion meditation will also help you to self-soothe.

As you start to feel better, you may be able to look at the situation differently. When we're caught up in the flames of anger it is hard to see the bigger picture. Once the flames have died down you may have a different perspective. So, check the facts. Use the rational part of your brain now that your anger has dissipated. Even if you still feel the same way, cooling down the flames will help to prepare you to communicate mindfully in order to reconcile with whoever you're feeling anger towards. Thich Nhat Hanh recommends that once anger has dissolved, if you are ready to talk and have something positive to say, don't wait. Tell the other person as soon as you can.

Mindful speaking/Assertiveness

Once you're ready to speak to the other person, I recommend using mindful speaking or assertiveness. When we fall out with people, we often feel the urge to bury our heads in the sand, hiding away from reality and hoping that the situation will somehow resolve itself. This doesn't do us or the other person any favours, as we end up stewing in our emotions and adding more stories to the ones already in our heads, and potentially exacerbating the situation. Once our anger has dissipated, we need to make an effort to reconcile. Mindful speaking or assertiveness can help you to express how you feel in a calm way while, at the same time, setting boundaries for what you will and won't accept in your relationship with the other person. This is done in a way that avoids coming across as aggressive or passive aggressive.

Jon Kabat-Zinn writes, "*What assertiveness training amounts to is mindfulness of feelings, speech and actions…[it] concerns your deepest ability to know yourself and to read situations appropriately and face them consciously.*"[22]

How do we practice assertiveness? A key element of assertiveness is making "I" statements rather than "You" statements. Problems can arise

---

22 Jon Kabat-Zinn, 2013, *Full Catastrophe Living: How to cope with stress, pain and illness using mindfulness meditation*, Piatkus, p491.

when you ignore or discount your own feelings or when you overreact to your feelings with aggression. Assertiveness involves communicating your feelings effectively. "I" statements communicate your feelings and opinions without blaming the other person for your feelings. For example, you might say, "*I feel so angry when you do X*" rather than "*You make me so angry*". In this "I" statement, you become accountable for your own feelings rather than pointing the finger at the other person, thus causing the other person to feel less attacked.

Before you communicate how you feel, make sure that you check in with your breathing. Use the breath to pause, step back and then speak. Trust me, it can help you to avoid blurting out a reaction, such as '*Just ******* leave me alone!!!*', rather than a response, such as '*I need some space right now to breathe*'. Mindful breathing will help you to gather yourself and then respond mindfully.

Dr Christopher Willard,[23] a psychologist and educational consultant who leads mindfulness and mental health workshops, uses a very helpful acronym: THINK. Ask yourself the following questions…

T: Is what I want to say **true**?

H: Is what I want to say **helpful**?

I: Am **I** the best one to say it?

N: Is it **necessary** to say it now?

K: Is it **kind** to this person and others?

Furthermore, Willard recommends that sometimes not saying anything at all or simply saying "*I don't know*" can be the most appropriate response. After all, sometimes we don't need to intellectualise what others are saying. Instead, we just need to listen with our whole hearts.

There is a place for anger and sometimes we have things to be genuinely angry about: Greta Thunberg's genuine anger at politician's lack of commitment to climate change measures, anger at misogyny, racism, injustice, etc. Such anger can be turned into action. But the anger we feel towards ourselves, and our family and friends, and others, is often due to other underlying issues (unmet needs) and we can use mindfulness to deal with that.

23 Christopher Willard, PsyD, 2014, *Mindfulness for teen anxiety: a workbook for overcoming anxiety at home, at school & everywhere else*, New Harbinger Publications, Inc. p113.

Chapter 10

Handling the ups and downs of dating

Tom: The Creep (A note I found stuffed into my diary, aged 15 in 1998)

We met at Penstowe. Then we went to a ball together on Valentine's Day and we had such a good time. We went around as if we were a couple and acted as if we were. People said we looked great together and I had never had such a great night out. I felt wanted and special. He said sweet things to me. Then he said that the words of the song 'Wonderwall' were like him saying it to me. He said he really liked me.

On the Monday after that I found out another girl, Jessica, from my school had snogged him after I had left. He rang up and apologised. I forgave him cos I really liked him. He was also extremely drunk.

After a month of ringing now and again we haven't seen each other. He hasn't rung. I really like him. I mean REALLY. I have been crying all the time at school and home over him. He just stopped ringing.

I plucked up the courage to ring him. I asked if he would have rung eventually, he said 'yes'. We spoke of meeting up but nothing got arranged. He hasn't rung all week. Laura, a mate, told me that he pulled someone else last weekend.

I cried again. I am crying. It is the end of the weekend and I think he probably pulled last night. I went to Penstowe hoping he would be there but no such luck.

I really hate the thought of him saying all these lovely things to another girl that he said to me.

He is a Scorpio, I am an Aries. Scorpio = fiery. Aries = fiery. BAD COMBINATION. TOO MUCH FIRE.

I am going to sleep now. Hopefully, I will stop crying as he couldn't care less. I had planned that we would go out, I would meet his parents, fat chance.

Ugh. The quest for love…what a minefield. It can be so exciting when you find someone special…it can be all rainbows and sunshine for a while. When it's all bright and positive we can often daydream future scenarios in our heads, making up moments which bring us even closer to that special someone. We let our imaginations run away with us as we walk through life with a happy theme tune playing in our heads. We act as if nothing else matters in the world but this one person, the person who makes us giddy and lifts us up, this person who will somehow sprinkle magic over any dark cloud. Oh, the high we feel when we meet someone new. It's so exciting and different.

And then at some point the rainbows and sunshine disappear for a while. Something painful arises – he likes someone else, you get stood up, you find out he's told all his friends what you get up to (maybe he's made it up), or he's boring and doesn't want to do any of the fun things you'd imagine doing with a boyfriend in those stories in your head. And the list goes on. The quest to find that special someone is messy and complicated.

If we really like them it can be very painful when we realise those moments will never happen as we had imagined. It is hard to believe that we will ever feel better…and yet, in time, we do. How can you mindfully handle heartache? With lots and lots of self-compassion. A mindful self-compassion meditation can help to release the heart-wrenching pain knotted within you. It can help to soothe you, meeting your pain with tenderness and warmth.

So, let those tears fall. Don't hold back. You may need to practice this meditation many times before the tears run dry. But start now. Let it all out. The more you let out the better. Listen to sad music for a while. You know, the music that makes you sob. Comfort yourself with a blanket. Hold yourself in a container of compassion. You can be there for yourself. For this moment will pass. Your ache will ease as the days and weeks go by. Know that you're not the only one in the world experiencing heartache right now, others out there are going through the same thing. See 'Meditations' section from page 115 to 146.

You can and you will get through it. Another person will come your way when the time is right. But more than this, learn that you don't need another person to complete you. You are enough just as you are. Your world will piece itself back together bit by bit. You may even come out of this realising that you were better off without that person. That is the beauty of time and self-love.

Asking someone out

I've written about handling heartache, what about other emotions that you can feel when you fancy someone? What if you want to ask someone out, but fear rejection? How do you even get up the nerve to ask someone out? Just thinking about it may spark the fight or flight response within you…your belly starts to flip, your palms get sweaty, your heart starts racing. This is fear in full force, as you play out the worst-case scenarios of rejection and embarrassment in your head.

Maybe you make up lots of stories where the situation doesn't pan out as you intended. As I have mentioned many times in this book, mindfulness can help you to become more aware of when you're indulging in your own rumour mill. Conscious breathing can help you to remain centred and check in with the facts, rather than the stories you're telling yourself about what could go wrong. Check in with your breathing as you consider the options of how to approach your desire. This will turn down the fight/flight stress response (in this case, the urge to run a thousand miles away!) and instead ignite the rest and digest system to signal to the body that everything is ok. I recommend trying the STOP technique on page 60 to calm your nerves before you ask someone out.

What if he/she says no?

If the person you've asked out says no, try tuning into your breathing and smile. You can be the mountain in that moment. You can handle the icy wind of rejection. You can remain rooted to the ground and confident in your own worth. You can choose to say "*Ok, no worries*" or something equally light in language that suits you, to remain calm and confident. After all, everyone has a choice and there are plenty of other people who will be attracted to you in your life.

But if you feel like your confidence has taken a hit, how about trying a mini self-soothing meditation, such as the 3-step breathing space on page 63. The 3-step breathing space meditation can help to soothe you if you're still out and about with other people around you. You just need to find a quiet, uninterrupted space for a few minutes to practice it. (And, yes, that may be in the toilet!).

When you get home, why not try a longer meditation to handle your emotions? The self-compassion meditation can help during times of rejection. We all experience rejection from time to time, so it is important that we learn how to handle those moments with compassion towards ourselves. Get your emotions out mindfully so that you're ready for the next opportunity that comes your way. Perhaps someone else takes your fancy or someone else approaches you. Your romantic world is likely to change frequently during your teenage years, those waves will keep coming, so learn how to surf them with self-compassion and a little bit of patience (tricky, I know!). See 'Meditations' from page 115 to 146.

Some of us can take years to find that special someone who we get to call 'boyfriend' or 'girlfriend'. There will be times in your life when you're not in a relationship. Use mindfulness to accept yourself as you are without the need for anyone else to validate you. Remember the mountain meditation or the self-acceptance meditation to boost your self-esteem. You are enough just as you are and the more you practice these meditations the more you will begin to realise this. See 'Meditations' from page 115 to 146.

Turning someone down mindfully

What about those moments when you are the one rejecting someone else? How can you do this while being mindful of their feelings? You can probably guess what to do by now…take a conscious breath before you say anything! This gives you a few seconds to pause and consider the other person's feelings in that moment. If you think about it, this person has taken a great deal of courage to come up to you and ask you out. Who knows how long he or she has prepared for this moment? Remember to be gentle with other people's hearts. Always be kind. The aim is to avoid blurting out something hurtful when the other person is showing vulnerability. By tuning into your breathing, you may find a more compassionate way to respond. Trust me, you will feel better about it in the long run if you turn someone down mindfully. Otherwise, your conscience could get the better of you by attacking you in the night for not showing compassion. You know, that little voice that reminds you of who you really are. Your words matter, so tune into your breathing if you feel like you're about to blurt something out that may harm another person. It can help you to respond mindfully, protecting the other person from harm and remaining true to who you really are.

Be gentle with the heart. This goes for other people's hearts but also your own. The quest to find that special someone is a mix of highs and lows. Relationships are complicated and messy at times. Use mindfulness to accept that you can't control other people's emotions, desires or actions. Use mindful self-compassion to handle all the emotions that surface from within you. Above all, remember that you are enough just as you are. You don't need another person to validate you. Use the self-acceptance meditation or mountain meditation to keep boosting your confidence and to help you remain true to yourself throughout.

Chapter 11

Social media

Friday 3rd January, 1997 – Did some French revision. Chris rang. His mates were in the background. He always rings from a phone box. He's spent about £4 on phone calls! Mum and dad don't like him phoning so much. I don't know how to tell him.

Sunday 5th January 1997 – Chris rang. He wants me to write to him, I must try and write tomorrow. Shall I go out with him?

Thursday 9th January, 1997 – I want Chris to ring me. I rang up and said to tell him I rang but he hasn't rung me back! He will have got his letter by now. I bet he hates it.

This was teenage life back in the 90's, BEFORE social media. If you liked someone you had to pluck up the courage to ring them on a landline. If you tried to call them you also had to deal with parents or siblings potentially picking up first, adding further embarrassment to the situation! You had to have an actual conversation on the phone rather than a quick exchange of messages. If you wrote them a letter you had to wait for days or weeks hoping that they would write back to you. You wouldn't get the quick signals that we can receive today, such as being unfollowed or blocked on social media. Things were different in the 90's. The absence of social media back then serves to highlight how ubiquitous it is today.

Let's face it, your phone is attached to your hip, or the palm of your hand, at all times. It keeps you connected with your friendship group, so you check it often. You may even sleep with it under your pillow! After all, you're part of a society that nurtures instant gratification. You're used to being plugged in all the time with information and entertainment available to you whenever you want (apart from when your parents restrict your usage). You can't help this urge to be plugged in. When you use social media, your brain releases **the addictive feel-good hormone, dopamine**. With a feel-good hit available to you in an instant, of course you're going to want more. It can catch you in a tailspin, allowing you to easily fall into the trap of hanging your self-esteem on every 'like' as a form of validation.

Why not try bringing more mindful awareness to your use of social media. According to author Cal Newport[24], 'social snacking' is starting to replace deeper human interactions. This has a negative effect on our wellbeing as we compare other people's social media status to our own. Other people's over-exaggerated, filtered, superficial social media status with our own over-exaggerated, filtered, superficial social media status. It is a competitive world of fakery, as we compete for who has captured the best sunset, the best pout, the best butt shot, the best squat pose, and so on. Yet we can't help it. It is so easy to get sucked in, because that dopamine high is powerful.

Therefore, it is all the more important that we bring mindful awareness to our consumption of social media, as we are more affected by it than we realise. This is particularly the case for teenagers, as your brains are geared towards social acceptance. So, of course social media is very important to you.

Approaching social media use with mindful awareness

How about paying more attention to what your body is up to? Your body is your emotional gauge and it will give you early warning signals if it feels overwhelmed by a stress response. For example, how do you feel when you check Snapchat in the morning? Do you check it calmly

---

24 Cal Newport, 2020, 'Digital Clutter' from The Minimalists Podcast, https://www.youtube.com/watch?v=oxr85CKSZNQ interviewed by Joshua Fields Millburn and Ryan Nicodemus. Ep.173.

or does your tummy flip a little at the prospect of what you may find? What are your shoulders up to? Have they already tensed? How about your jaw? Your body may be giving you signals that you're more stressed about it than you realise.

And what is your brain up to? Are you making up stories? If FOMO is at play, you may already feel tense about conversations you possibly missed overnight or worse, conversations that may have been deleted. You may even go so far as to imagine worst case scenarios playing out at school because you missed a conversation. You may have a constant hideous feeling of doom sitting on your shoulders.

Being more aware of what your body and mind are up to can help you to realise how social media is affecting you. If you notice the automatic stress response creeping in, I advise that you take a few conscious breaths to anchor yourself in the here and now. Then decide if you really need to go onto social media right now or if you would benefit from doing something else that will provide a healthy release to your tension. This release could be through meditation, exercise, baking, playing with your dog, being creative…whatever you need that allows you to healthily release your stress, rather than throwing yourself into a conversation or newsfeed that may only cause you more stress.

What about your mood during and after social media use? Do you feel good or do you feel a bit…empty? We often experience low moods after hours of scrolling and absorbing other people's perfectly filtered photos and perfectly fake lives. I too have been guilty of mindless scrolling in the past when I have forgotten to mindfully approach social media. Since 2015, there have been numerous studies on the negative impacts of social media[25]. The results indicate that frequent social media use causes feelings of anxiety, isolation, low self-esteem and poor sleep.

Therefore, consider how long you spend on social media each day and whether the content you're consuming makes you feel happy or unhappy.

---

25   Janet Street-Porter, 2016, 'Social media is making us depressed: let's learn to turn it off' https://www.independent.co.uk/voices/social-media-is-making-us-depressed-lets-learn-to-turn-it-off-a6974526.html

Waking up to the present

You're the generation experiencing things faster than ever. The speed at which you consume information and entertainment is staggering. Trends are constantly changing. With apps such as TikTok there is always a new trend to be aware of. No wonder we're facing a teenage mental health crisis, as your brains struggle to keep up. The overstimulation must be exhausting.

I encourage you to take a break from social media every now and then. When something beautiful happens in your life, how about stopping to take in the moment as it is? Rather than filming the moment or taking a photo and adding a filter, how about just enjoying the moment? I can already hear you gasp at the idea of not sharing your experience with everyone! It has become so engrained in us to capture and share every moment of our lives. We have become so preoccupied with our social media status that we forget to fully experience the moment. We forget to experience the world as it is, and fail to notice what is truly happening around us. As the digital revolution speeds up even more, the stress of adjusting to it will only increase. We really need to pay more attention to life as it is right now. As Jon Kabat-Zinn[26] says, "*…we get pulled out of ourselves and wind up losing sight of what is most important…*"

Taking in the good

As I noted in Chapter 2, we are far more likely to store negative experiences in the brain than positive ones. A 'Taking in the good' exercise involves learning to rest our attention on the positive for a while. This helps us to handle stress better, boosting the immune system and increasing overall happiness.

So, why not give it a go? Spend the next 30 seconds recalling a memory that makes you happy. Bring all of your senses to it. What did it look like? How did it smell? What could you touch? What could you hear? Was there a taste attached to it? Tune into all the emotions that are stirred up by that memory and savour them.

When the practice has ended, notice how you feel. Now try to do this

---

26 Jon Kabat-Zinn, 2013, *Full Catastrophe Living: How to cope with stress, pain and illness using mindfulness meditation*, Piatkus, pxl.

practice based on your experiences in the present. The next time you notice an amazing sunset or your pet does something super cute, really savour that experience for what it is, rather than rushing to capture it and share it.

Conscious breathing and creating social media boundaries

Before you post something on social media, how about pausing first? Take a few conscious breaths and then consider what you're hoping to gain from it…a certain number of likes? Ask yourself how many likes will be enough to feel validated? That spike of dopamine won't last very long. It is a game you can't win as you battle over and over to achieve that dopamine hit again. It is exhausting and unhealthy. And what happens when you're not validated with likes? How does that make you feel? I know that some teenagers will take down a picture within 15 minutes if it doesn't receive enough likes. This is not good for you. If you think a picture is good enough then it is good enough as it is. It may sound alien to you, but you don't need anyone else to validate it for you. I understand this may be too much to ask of you as your brains are hardwired towards social acceptance, so perhaps before you post, consider how you're feeling. If you're already feeling a bit low and then post something which doesn't achieve the level of validation you were looking for, you could end up feeling worse. So, look after your mental health and tune into how you're truly feeling. If you are feeling down, then I recommend taking a step back from social media for a while until you feel better. Research has already shown us that social media can create a low mood, so remember to be more mindful of how and when you use it. You need to comfort yourself in the appropriate way if you're feeling low. A self-compassion meditation might be just what you need instead of social media. See 'Meditations' from page 115 to 146. After you have practiced self-compassion (the short, 3-step breathing space, version of the meditation, if you don't have time for the longer one), see if you still want to post on social media. Who knows how you may feel after a little mindfulness?

Overcoming the stress caused by social media

If you start to feel the tremors of stress bubbling up while you're using social media, why not try the STOP technique on page 60 as a coping strategy? Another way to approach social media in a more mindful way is by remembering that you can create boundaries whenever you need to. You have the choice to unfollow anyone at any time. Don't waste time following someone who brings you down. Look after yourself. If anyone is causing you pain via social media unfollow them or block them. Seriously, you don't need more drama in your life. Unfollow or block whoever is bringing you negativity so that you no longer allow them into your social media space.

Trolling

It would be remiss of me to not discuss trolling. Social media can get very nasty very quickly and, tragically, can cause some to end their lives because of the abuse they receive.

Remember the marshmallow incident in Chapter 7? Sometimes people act out of character. Are you trolling, being mean online or engaging in online bullying just because everyone else is doing it? Are you doing it because of the potential anonymity that you are assured? Are you doing it in the hope that the trolls won't pick on you next?

I ask you to be mindful of the words that you use. Ask yourself if you would ever say this to someone's face? If you wouldn't, then why would you post it or message it? If that doesn't resonate, consider those closest to you. How would they feel if they received the message that you're thinking of sending? Imagine someone that you genuinely care for…your sister, mum, brother, dad, your best friend. How much pain would your post or message cause them? Seriously, how much pain? Do you want to be responsible for all those tears? Ask yourself, deep down, are you really that person? Consider where this urge to troll has come from…is this your own pain and frustration at the world? Does this feeling stem from an unmet emotional need? Is it a feeling you don't know how to handle, a feeling that bites at you, that gnaws at you deep down in your belly? Is it a fire of anger that burns so strongly from the pain you're experiencing that you want to release it onto someone else, with your anger in full force?

Maybe you're trolling out of anger. There's nothing wrong with being angry. Sometimes we have very good reason to be angry. In Chapter 9, I provided you with tools to help you to release your anger in a healthy way. Every day, you have a new opportunity to be a kinder person. I believe that most of us have it in us to be kind if we take the time to work on ourselves. We need to build self-awareness, unearth those unmet needs, acknowledge them and accept them for what they are. Then we can use healthy coping strategies such as mindfulness and self-compassion to allow our true, kinder nature to come through. Dig deep, then dig again. You can unearth a kinder, more compassionate you. You just need to be kinder and more compassionate with yourself first.

Thich Nhat Hanh advises that we never speak when we're angry. It only causes more pain for everyone. In today's world, I suggest that also means that we never post or message when angry. Never. It's not worth it. Trust me. It may cause more pain than you had imagined. You don't know how long your words may stay with someone. Your words could cause irreparable damage. Look at what happened to Caroline Flack. You never know what is truly going on in someone's life. Don't be the person who could tip someone over the edge.

If you're frustrated with your life right now, remember that it will change. And when your life changes, you may look back and regret what you said or did. You can't take back the words once they're out there. So, remember to be more mindful in your use of social media. Deal with your pain, sit with your pain, go inward and understand yourself. That person you want to hurt with your words…ask yourself, what have they actually done to you personally? Really consider this question. This is pain within you that has come from elsewhere and you can release it if you choose to.

Bobby Norris's campaign #endthetrend2troll is shifting awareness of this topic. Having been trolled himself, he uses his fame to raise awareness of the problem. He is campaigning to put an end to trolling once and for all. His words, 'Think before you type' really resonate here. So please, think before you type.

Sleep

Give yourself some time before bed (ideally an hour) when you do something you enjoy that takes you away from your phone. This could be having a bath, listening to music, playing with a pet, practising yoga…

whatever helps you to wind down and unplug. Numerous studies confirm that screen time before bed can play havoc with your sleep patterns. The more shut eye you get the easier it will be to face whatever is coming your way the next day.

Social media is a huge part of our lives. We are plugged in all the time. The place that we plug into needs to be a place of love, positivity, kindness, warmth and compassion. Let's also make social media a more positive place. Social media is here to stay, but it doesn't have to get in the way of real experiences, and we should use it mindfully and with kindness and compassion.

Chapter 12

Handling illness or grief

Tuesday 18th November, 1997 – I've heard some really bad news. Jane, a girl at my school has been taken to hospital after severe headaches and is unconscious. I think it's terrible. She'll probably get better though, I hope.

Wednesday 19th November, 1997 – Jane has got better. She had a blood clot in the brain. Didn't do much homework. Watched TV. I don't have the motivation.

Thursday 20th November, 1997 – We've heard some terrible news, Jane has died. I can't take it in. I mean, the last thing I said to her was that her skirt looked nice and she was laughing about something. She was younger than me. We had an assembly for her. Everyone was crying.

Friday 28th December, 1997 – I went to Jane's funeral. It was so sad. It was lovely though. Her uncle sang a beautiful song of farewell. It really touched my emotions.

Jane was a popular girl at my school, liked by a lot of people. She had a warm, smiley and caring presence. It was scary and painful when she passed away, and I didn't even know her that well. Pain is pain. You don't have to be especially close to someone to miss them when they're gone. So, if you can feel pain when someone you don't know too well passes away, what about having to handle news about someone closer?

When you hear devastating news about a loved one, whether a friend, a family member, or your beloved pet, you feel a stabbing feeling in your heart like no other. The news may be that they've been diagnosed with a frightening illness, been in an accident or passed away. Whatever the Earth-shattering news, it engulfs your entire being. A storm surrounds you. A storm that is ugly, brutal and dark, with no clear blue sky in sight.

Unfortunately, heart-breaking news doesn't wait until the time is right to slap you across the face. It can turn up at any time, even during the most stressful periods of your life, such as exam season.

How can you handle painful news about a loved one?

When I heard the news that my 37-year old friend's cancer was back and had spread around her body, I felt so angry, heart-broken and helpless. I had to come to terms with the fact that her lifespan would be dramatically shortened. I had to learn to accept that there were only so many special moments left between us, and only so many special moments left for her and her beautiful family and other loved ones. The news was hard to swallow. You expect your friends to be around until you're both really old. You don't expect them to leave the world early. You don't expect them to have to withstand the hideous suffering that cancer brings.

In an interview on 'How to care deeply about others without burning out', Sharon Salzberg and Dan Harris discuss the importance of balance. "*…There is a balance that's really crucial…you can acknowledge the suffering, you can want to help, but you recognise that you can't solve everything…*"[27]

This quote resonated with me at the time. Not only was I sad about the uncertainty of how long more I would get to share the world with her, I was also on a hamster wheel of thoughts about what my friend was going through, how she was dealing with every day, the physical and emotional pain she was experiencing, and how her family was coping.

When I read that quote, I realised that I could only do so much for her. I could offer to help. I could listen. I could be at the end of a phone call

27 Sharon Salzberg and Dan Harris, 2017, 'How to care deeply without burning out', https://www.mindful.org/care-deeply-without-burning-out/

or Facetime or WhatsApp. I could visit her whenever it suited her. I could acknowledge the downright hideousness of the situation. But I could not make her cancer go away, as much as it pained me to acknowledge this.

Realising that there is only so much I could do for my friend was a hard pill to swallow. Realising that I had to accept some truths in order to look after myself and my dear friend better was also a hard pill to swallow.

The above quote helped me to realise that I wasn't being compassionate with myself. Deep down I was internalising feelings of guilt. Guilt that my body was healthy, guilt that I could go about my life without the pull of physical pain holding me back, guilt that I could make future plans with my family and friends without having to question if I would be around for them.

So, consider this question, are you being compassionate with yourself right now? Remember, if you don't release the pain in a healthy way it may bottle up and come to the surface later in life, perhaps as anger or some other extreme reaction. Swallowing emotions can also make you feel ill. Too much stress affects the immune system, making you more likely to pick up nasty illnesses. It can also affect other relationships that you hold dear. If you're holding onto tension it can build inside you like a pressure cooker ready to explode at the slightest thing. The pain is likely to come out in an unhealthy way, in a way that you may regret. So, remember to really look after yourself when devastating news hits your life. Mindful self-compassion needs to be your default. This is the time to be super compassionate with yourself. I recommend that you try a self-compassion meditation to start releasing pain in a healthy way, little by little. Make sure that you pick a time when you can rest after you have listened to and practiced the meditation. It is natural to feel drained after releasing so much pain. See 'Meditations' from page 115 to 146.

Be with your feelings for a while

When I heard the news about my friend, my instant reaction was to cry and talk about it with my husband over and over again. The important thing was to let the feelings out and not suppress them. We went on a drive to the beach to get some fresh air and a change of scene. On the drive, my husband intentionally played sombre music to help my feelings come to the surface. It was important that I took some time to just be with the pain, releasing it bit by bit. If listening to sombre music helps you to release those emotions, then listen to the music that works for you. Self-soothing can really help during this time and, as we can often feel cold when we're sad or drained, remember to wrap yourself in a blanket or duvet or place a hand on your heart for comfort and warmth. Or if music doesn't help, you could go for a walk to get fresh air and release some of the pent-up frustration and raw emotion you are experiencing. Do whatever works for you during this painful time and allow yourself to wallow for a while. With so much pain to handle, you owe it to yourself to take care of yourself during this difficult time.

Handling grief

Grief is yet another level of pain. A few months ago, when I heard that my friend had passed away, I wrote down how it felt:

> *Enduring gnawing at the heart. It feels tight. It feels like it is squeezing. I look up at the sky and talk to her. Tears readily appear, blurring my vision. I see a flock of birds performing a dance in the sky. Can I hear her giggling at this? I smile and feel a bit better. I manage to get up and get on with some things. I get into it and let go. Something makes me laugh. Then I catch myself. I remember again. The overwhelming heaviness engulfs me again. She is gone. Silence. Reality. The sun shines on my face. I feel warmth. Is she there? I tell myself she is. It is coming from somewhere peaceful. She is content. I will be content again…one day.*

Here are some tips which may help you to handle the enormity of grief:

- Take each day as it comes. Grief's road is different for everyone. Some will return to a new normality quicker than others. We're all different. Some days, you'll be ok and manage to get by without crumbling to the floor in a heap. Other days, you'll just about get through the day, get home and weep for hours.

There is no right way to grieve. As long as you're looking after yourself healthily, by looking after your eating and sleeping patterns, and being compassionate with yourself, then you're getting through. You're surfing those waves of grief, so pat yourself on the back for carrying on.

- Be patient with yourself and with the whole grieving process. One of the key attributes of mindfulness is patience. Every time you feel your legs go weak when you hear a song that reminds you of your lost loved one, be patient with yourself. Every time you see a photo on social media that sends daggers to your heart, be patient with yourself. Grief's road is different for everyone. Of course, it's going to hurt. Even weeks, months, years down the line it may still hurt. The pain will return every now and then because you hold a little piece of your loved one in your heart. This is ok. In fact, this is a beautiful thing. But, over time, it will get easier to carry on. If you give yourself the time you deserve to truly release the pain, you'll find that you start to feel better. There is no timetable for grief. Just be kind to yourself as you go through the process of acceptance. Do not shy away from the hard bits.

- Be gentle with your heart. In the long run, swallowing your feelings won't work. Don't try to lock your pain away in your body. You have the key to unlock your emotions. If you try to suppress your pain it is likely to come back to haunt you later in life…most likely as anger (fuelled by an unmet emotional need). Your emotional need right now is to be heard, acknowledged, accepted in every way. If you are dealing with grief, I highly recommend that you meditate regularly. If you feel heartache burning in your chest, try letting it out through a mindful self-compassion meditation.

- We rarely grieve alone. We're often in a house full of grief – as a teenager, you may have lost your grandparent, but so have your siblings, your own parent has lost their mum or dad. Be compassionate not only to yourself, but also to your fellow grievers, who will all deal with it differently, and who will all have their very own personal memories and loss. The grief isn't yours alone.

- Be honest with your friends. You don't have to wear a mask, pretending that everything is ok. Your friends know everything is not ok and that it won't feel ok for some time. Be true to yourself during this time. Your true friends will be there for you as you weather this storm.

If you don't always have time for the full self-compassion meditation, try a mini meditation, such as the 3-step breathing space on **page 63**, to soothe you for a few minutes.

Chapter 13

Building deeper connections, truly being there for each other

This final chapter is about opening out, using mindfulness to connect with other people. Having gone inside to feel compassion and acceptance for yourself, and to gain self-knowledge, you are now moving outwards again, to engage with others mindfully and with compassion.

We can all feel out of the friendship group from time to time. Even adults can feel that way! We can sometimes feel misunderstood or left out of a conversation for whatever reason. We often take it very personally without knowing the full context of the situation. Perhaps, as I discussed in Chapter 3, the other person is dealing with something big that you are unaware of.

In order to build solid relationships with others we need to learn how to communicate well so that we can fully understand each other. Good listening is an essential part of communication. Sometimes the person with the biggest smile is hiding the most pain. Do not be fooled by the smile, it may be masking an ocean of tears. I invite you to check in with your friends and family, not just once, but regularly. You never know what is really going on until you stop what you are doing, ask the question, take a breath and listen with your whole heart. Then pause and listen again. To be heard can make an enormous difference to someone's day. In some cases, it can make someone's year. It can turn things around in ways you may never know.

Listening with your whole heart

How can you listen with your whole heart? I mean listening fully, really focussing on what the other person is saying without thinking about what you're going to say next. I mean putting aside your own agenda (your own internal running commentary that may be adding judgement along the way).

Here are some skills to help you…

The first step to mindful listening or 'deeply listening', as Thich Nhat Hanh calls it, is to stop what you're doing. You need to put down that device. Yes, I'm referring to your phone. The thing that sits next to you at the dinner table. The thing that rests on the sofa beside you. The thing that goes to the toilet with you (don't lie, I know you do this!). The thing that NEVER LEAVES YOUR SIDE. Put it down. Even just having a phone by your side can make the other person feel unheard if they're speaking to you. Have your parents ever got frustrated with you because you're still on your phone while they're talking to you? It's because you're not really listening to them. So please, if a friend or family member really needs to be heard, put the phone down, whatever is going on in that world can wait. If you have something on your mind that needs attention, quickly pop it in your phone as a reminder and then silence it, because any pings, swooshing sounds or whatever else goes on when others are trying to contact you will distract from the conversation with the person right in front of you.

Second, ensure that you're mindfully ready. Are you grounded right now or do you need to take a few mindful breaths before you start? It is worth ensuring that you're feeling alright before you start listening to others. Take a few conscious breaths to anchor yourself in the here and now, to ensure that you're fully present for the other person.

Third, consider your body language. Are you positioning yourself in an open way to fully listen to the other person? I mean are you facing them? This may sound obvious, but both of you may be seated facing outwards. If so, turn and face the other person. Now consider your arms… are they placed in a warm, open and friendly manner i.e. placed on your lap or by your side? You want to avoid crossed arms as that can signal a closed, disinterested attitude. How about your face? Are you maintaining eye contact (without freaking the other person out by staring and not blinking)? What is your face up to? My face has given my feelings away many times before. I've assumed that the other person can't sense what I am thinking as I have listened patiently with no interruptions but then wondered why they've stopped talking. My face was giving away the fact that I was distracted and busy in my own thoughts. Or that I was showing my judgement with a flicker of an eyebrow or a frown – facial movements that I was unaware of! So, try to be more aware of your facial expressions to encourage the other person to fully open up.

Fourth, keep tuning into your breathing. This will help you to notice when you are becoming judgemental or distracted, allowing you to pause, acknowledge the thought, then connect fully with the other person again. This helps you to guide yourself back to the present moment over and over. So, take a mindful breath or two whenever you feel yourself being pulled away from the conversation.

Fifth, respond warmly. A nod from time to time or an agreeing '*hmmm*' can really help. For the person talking it can feel very strange to 'have the floor', to have someone's full attention for so long, so it helps to know that the other person is still listening rather than getting bored or distracted. Keep an eye on your tone of voice as you respond, so that you remain warm and friendly.

Sixth, try to not interrupt. This can be really hard if you enjoy chatting! If you interrupt, you are taking the other person off track, you are steering the conversation down a different track that is not their track. This is not the purpose of mindful listening. Mindful listening is about them, not you. It takes a lot of practice and it is something I still struggle with from time to time. Pure listening requires listening with your whole heart, which means opening your heart to other people's truths and listening to their story. You may find that some comments trigger strong emotions inside of you. Again, use breathing as your anchor. Breathing will ground you in the present moment, it will help you to handle your emotions so that you can completely be there for the other person.

Seventh, and perhaps most important, is that once the other person has finished talking you may not need to say anything at all. You don't have to intellectualise the problem. You don't have to fix anything. Your role in this scenario is to listen. You could say "*I'm glad that you told me*" or "*That sounds so painful*" or give them a hug if it feels appropriate (not everyone likes this). But just being there and listening holds the most power.

Take care of yourself

You owe it to yourself to regularly check in on your mental health. With tragedies such as the death of Caroline Flack creating shockwaves across social media, we are reminded more than ever to take better care of ourselves.

Stress manifests itself within the body in numerous ways and it is up to each one of us to pay more attention to ourselves. Your body is your emotional gauge, so start listening to its cues. The body doesn't lie. You know the feeling when you're trying to make everything look ok? Smiling and holding your head up high, but your chest is tight or your tummy is flipping or your shoulders feel like they're attached to your ears. Your body is saying *'Hello?! You can't ignore this feeling forever. You need to mindfully meditate…sit with me, lie with me or move with me to start acknowledging some of these feelings. They're not going away until you pay more attention.'* The body doesn't lie. Listen to it.

When you use meditations such as the Body Scan and the Breathing meditation you can connect with the body more, identifying where you're holding on to tension. When you start to release it healthily, you turn down the fight or flight stress reaction and ignite the rest and digest system that says to the body *'Everything is ok'*.

Mindful self-compassion will add to the healing process by soothing any tension or heavy emotions you have unearthed. It helps you to be there for yourself. Use a self-compassion meditation whenever you feel unsteady, whenever those emotions are bubbling up inside of you, making you want to scream at your parents or siblings. Those emotional needs are calling to be held in a container of compassion. If you ignore them by trying to swallow them, you may start to feel the heat of anger rising up in your body. It may unleash a beast that knows no boundaries, taking down anyone in its path, hurting those closest to you with daggers that cut deep. Be more compassionate with yourself, dig deep and understand what is really going on inside of you. This is where the healing begins. Step forward and start taking responsibility for your own mental health.

The Mountain meditation will boost your confidence further by grounding you at home before you step out into the world. As you start to listen to yourself better and practice these techniques more often your resilience will start to increase. Events that may have previously triggered knee-jerk reactions may no longer ignite you in the same way. Of course, you may still be affected, you just have tools to help you to handle those feelings healthily. These are tools that you can turn to whenever you need them, surfing whatever wave comes your way.

The more you turn towards yourself, the more you start to accept yourself as you are, validating yourself in your truest form, away from the glare of social media. Your true, beautiful self. Every. Single. Bit. Using positive self-talk rather than negative self-talk, unfollowing the people who bring you down, regularly making space for meditations, such as the self-acceptance meditation, that lift you up, trusting that you are totally enough just as you are. Transforming yourself from self-sabotage to self-love.

If nothing else remember Thich Nhat Hanh's words… *"Feelings come and go like clouds in a windy sky. Conscious breathing is my anchor."* Use this to ground yourself in the face of every challenge that comes your way. It will help you more than you can imagine. It will help prevent sudden reactions. It may save a friendship from a big falling out. It may save you from hurting your family. It can help you to handle stress and anxiety in the face of what often feels like endless school work. It can help you during exam season to gather yourself before the tests begin or during revision time to focus on the task at hand or when giving a presentation in front of your peers. Conscious breathing is truly your anchor, your home base, your best friend who will always keep you grounded. Don't forget about it. This is a tool you can use for the rest of your life. You are just one mindful breath away from a more centred, grounded you.

> *"Once we're thrown off our habitual paths, we think all is lost; but it's only here that the new and the good begins. As long as there's life, there's happiness. There's much, much still to come."*
>
> *War and Peace*, Leo Tolstoy[28]

---

28 Leo Tolstoy, 2007, *War and Peace*, translated by Richard Pevear and Larissa Volokhonsky, Vintage Books, London, p1118.

The Meditations

The Body Scan

Lie down comfortably on a mat or thick rug. Add a pillow if you want to and a blanket, as you may get cold during the practice. Place your arms down by your sides with your palms facing upwards. Legs slightly apart and feet relaxed. Make any extra adjustments now to ensure you're as comfortable as possible. This meditation involves focussing on different parts of the body moment by moment.

Remember there is no right way to feel, so try to accept whatever sensations come up moment by moment. It is also only natural that your mind will start to wander. Use the breath to anchor yourself back to the present. If you feel any discomfort in your body, try to approach with kindness and openness to soften the experience. The aim of this meditation is to fall awake so if you feel yourself drifting off to sleep, move your body a little to stay awake.

Now close your eyes and become aware of the breath flowing in and out of your body as it wants to…
No need to change the way you breathe…
Now rest attention on your feet…all of your awareness is on your feet…
How do they feel today? Can you feel any tingling? Are they warm or cool?

How about your toes, what sensations are here? Can you feel each toe separately?
Now imagine your awareness is slowly flowing down the arches of your feet right down to your heels…

All of your attention is now on your heels…
Can you feel the weight of your body pressing down here?
Now let awareness flow to the top of your feet…
What sensations lie here? Can you feel the blanket or your socks?

Now place your attention on your calves…
If you're lying on a mat, can you feel the weight pressing down on the mat?
Sensing and accepting with every breath…

Now let's bring awareness to your knees…
The front of your knees, the back of the knees…
Deep into the knee joints…
What are you sensing here?
If your mind wanders, gently focus on your breathing moment by moment.

From the knees let your attention travel up to your thighs…
Feeling the weight of your thighs resting on the mat…
Now take in the whole of your legs…
All your energy and focus are here, be with it, accept it as it is right now…
Notice all sensations in this moment…and then this moment…
Not judging, not striving, just being…

Now I invite you to rest attention on your hips…
The right hip, the left hip…
How do your hips feel?
Allow sensations to be just as you find them…

As we move to your buttocks…
The right buttock, the left buttock…
Is there any tension here in this moment? Then this moment?

How about your pelvis?
Can you imagine your breath flowing into your pelvis and out again?
Like the tide flowing in and out to the rhythm of your own breathing…

How about your abdomen, how does that feel?
Are you aware of your tummy rising and falling?
Perhaps rest a hand there if it helps…
If restless feelings come, remember to focus on the breath.

Then let your awareness flow up to your chest…
Feeling your rib cage rising and falling…
Perhaps you can feel your heart beating or your lungs expanding and collapsing with each breath…

Now let's move to your lower back…
Remembering to let your body be as it is in this moment…
Taking in each sensation with curiosity and openness…
Allowing your back to relax a little more with each breath…

Now let your awareness flow up the spine to the middle of the back…
Noticing any sensations here…
Then right up to the top of your back…
Now you're fully aware of the whole of your back…
Resting all your attention here, allowing, welcoming…
All your energy is here flowing up and down your spine…

Now let's rest attention on the shoulders…
Feel the weight of your shoulders…

Many of us carry emotions and tension here…
Are your shoulders feeling tight or relaxed?

Now take your attention to your hands…
To the tips of your fingers and thumbs…
Can you feel the space in between your fingers and your thumbs?

The palms of your hands…
Do they feel warm or cool?
Can you feel any tingling sensations?
What else can you feel here?

How about your wrists?
How do they feel?
Sensing with openness and kindness…

Now turn your attention to your forearms and your elbows…
What lies here in this moment?
Just accept and be with all sensations as they arise…

Now let your awareness flow to the top of your arms…
To your biceps, triceps…
Welcoming all feelings in this area of your body as you tune into your own breathing…

So now you're aware of the whole of your arms…
Resting attention here as you breathe in and out…

And let your awareness flow up to your neck…
A lot of tension can sit here so approaching with kindness and curiosity…
Accepting whatever you feel as you breathe in and out…

Now let's take in the throat…
What sensations lie here?
Be with them softly and gently…

Now let awareness flow up to your head…
Feel the heaviness of your head pressing down on the mat…
Be mindful of the facial muscles that we use every day…
Taking in the forehead, the temples, the ears…
The back of your face to your eyes…
The eye sockets…the eyelids…the eyebrows…the space between your eyebrows…
Feel the breath flowing through your nostrils…
The surface of the nose, the cheeks…
The lower jaw, relaxing any tension here…
The mouth, the lips…
Feel your tongue in your mouth…
Letting it move around the back of your teeth, your gums…
Imagining the breath flowing into the back of your face and out again…
Refreshing and reviving.

Now you're aware of your whole body resting peacefully…
Your full weight supported by the ground…
The whole of your body in tune with your breathing…
A flow of energy moving up and down your body…
Now just lie or sit here enjoying the stillness you have created.

Now start to wriggle your toes and fingers…
Stretch yours arms above your head and stretch your legs pointing the toes…
And gently, softly turn to your right side…
Sit up or stand up when you feel ready and open your eyes…
Congratulate yourself on taking time to just be with yourself.

The Breathing Meditation

Sit comfortably in an upright position with shoulders relaxed, chest open, feet flat on the floor.

Make any adjustments now to ensure you're as comfortable as possible.

Close your eyes and start paying attention to your breathing…

Tuning into your body in this moment…

Taking in the feet, lower legs, upper legs, hips, buttocks, noticing how it feels to be supported by the chair, sinking into the practice on each breath…

Then taking in the whole of your back, arms, shoulders, neck and finally head…

Become aware of the whole of your body sitting here breathing…

Now let your attention drop into wherever you feel the breath…

Perhaps in your tummy noticing how it feels as your tummy rises on the in-breath and drops on the out-breath…

Or perhaps you feel it more in the chest area…

Noticing how it feels as your ribcage expands on the in-breath and contracts on the out-breath…

Or maybe you feel it more in the nostrils…

Tuning into the feeling of each in-breath and out-breath in your nostrils and perhaps at the tip of your nose…

It may be cooler in an in-breath and warmer on an out-breath.

Wherever you feel it most, allow yourself to really tune into the rhythm of your own breathing…

Noticing how your breath ebbs and flows…

Like the tide coming in and out…

Flowing naturally in its own time…

Not striving, not competing, just being…

Becoming aware of any other sensations in the body as you sit here breathing moment by moment…

Approach these sensations with curiosity and openness…

If your mind becomes restless remember to be kind to yourself…

Imagine your mind is the sky and your thoughts are like clouds coming and going…

Each one new and different…

If you become swept up in worrying, planning, daydreaming try not to judge yourself…

Instead make a mental note and then let the thought cloud pass by…

Focussing back again on how it feels to breathe in your body in this moment…

Anchoring yourself back into the practice…

Dropping into wherever you feel the breath most naturally…

Seeing your in-breath as a new beginning and your out-breath as a release, let go of any tension you're holding onto. Thich Nhat Hanh says, "*Breathing in, I'm aware of my body, breathing out, I celebrate my body. Breathing in, I feel calm in my body. Breathing out I release the tension in my body.*"

Now practice by yourself using the silence provided…*(allow 1 minute to pass)*

Guiding yourself back to the breath as the mind wanders… *(allow 1 minute to pass)*

Gently and slowly start to become aware of your whole body again…

Noticing the sensations that arise from whatever you're in contact with…

Sensations on the surface or deep down inside your body… Now gently lower your chin and slowly open your eyes… Taking a few stretches to end the practice.

The Mountain Meditation

This meditation is adapted from Jon Kabat-Zinn's Mountain Meditation. It involves a seated position either on the floor with a cushion or bolster, or sitting on a chair.

We're going to start by grounding ourselves, taking attention to the feet and to how it feels to be supported by the ground. If sitting on a chair, notice how it feels to be supported by the chair.

Now, I invite you to tune into wherever you feel the breath most naturally in your body. This could be the rise and fall of your breathing in your tummy, or in your chest as you notice the rib cage expanding and contracting, or in your nostrils as you feel the sensation of every in-breath and every out-breath. Ground yourself in this practice.

Now, I invite you to picture in your head, the most beautiful mountain you can imagine. This could be something that you've seen before or something that you're imagining for the first time. Bring it to mind now. Notice its overall mass. A single lofty peak or several peaks high up in the sky. Notice its overall shape. Notice how steep the sides are. Perhaps there are trees around this mountain. Or maybe there is a lake nearby. Is there grass? Is there snow and ice? Or is it summer time? Or is the mountain wearing the fire colours of autumn? Is there a stream nearby or a waterfall? What can you hear? Are there birds overhead? Is there a breeze? Can you feel the breeze in your face? Or if there are trees perhaps you can notice the breeze in the trees? Are there clouds overhead?

Now I ask you to sense the base of this mountain which is grounded and rooted deep down into the earth's crust. This mountain isn't moving anywhere. This mountain is stable, solid. It isn't affected by the weather around it. It isn't affected by the seasons that change. It isn't affected by what people say when they come to see the mountain. Even when the mountain is clouded, when you can't even see it properly. This mountain is unmoved. Unmoved by the weather. Unmoved by appearances, because it remains at all times itself.

Rain will come. And winds. Very powerful winds. Trees will sway and yet the mountain remains solid. Rooted in the earth. Unmoved by what is happening around it.

When you are comfortable with this image in your head, I invite you to imagine bringing the mountain into your own body. Your head becomes the peak high up in the sky, your shoulders and arms become the sides of the mountain. Your buttocks and your legs, are the solid base rooted to the ground.

Just like the mountain, you are grounded in the earth. You are unmoved by the weather. By what's happening around you. By the seasons. By appearances around you. You can remain yourself at all times. Wind and rain and snow may come to push against your mountain, to challenge your mountain. Huge storms may appear. You can remain yourself regardless of the weather patterns around you. Seasons will change. The weather will change. And yet the mountain remains itself.

Notice how it feels in your body when you imagine yourself as this mountain. And remember you can tune into this feeling of being like a mountain whenever you want. Grounding yourself into the earth's crust. Feeling whole, complete, entirely yourself. Unmoved by the weather patterns and by the chaos of life around you.

When you are ready, I invite you to drop your chin to your chest, slowly open your eyes and have a good stretch. The practice is now complete.

Self-acceptance meditation

Welcome to the self-acceptance meditation. If you start to feel overwhelmed by emotions remember you can always come back to the breath to anchor yourself in the present. Remembering to always be kind to yourself.

Start by getting comfortable in a seated position either on a chair or on the floor. Feel free to get a blanket or cushions to ensure you're as comfortable as possible.

Ensure you have an upright posture with your spine straight, shoulders nice and relaxed, feet flat on the ground or legs crossed if on the floor. Lower your chin towards your chest and close your eyes…

I invite you to place a hand on your heart if that feels comfortable for you. Feel free to place it back down onto your lap whenever you want to.

Now close your eyes and let your attention drop to wherever you feel the breath most naturally…

This may be in your abdomen noticing your tummy rising and falling…

Or perhaps in the chest area noticing your ribcage expanding and contracting…

Or maybe you feel it more in the nostrils noticing the feeling of each in breath and out breath through your nostrils…

Wherever it feels most natural just be with it in this moment…

Gently connect with your body as you tune into your breathing…

Now I invite you to pay attention to your hand on your heart…

Notice the warmth of your hand resting gently on your body…

Perhaps how it moves gently along with your breath…

Now I invite you to ask yourself what you really need today, right here right now…

Perhaps you need love…

Perhaps you need kindness towards yourself or acceptance of who you are…

What do you really need?

If nothing comes to you, that's ok. We will repeat a few phrases now to help you tune into what you really need.

Let's start with *May I be kind to myself, truly kind to myself.*

Repeat the phrase in your head now…*May I be kind to myself, truly kind to myself.*

Or how about…*May I accept myself as I am.*

How does it feel in your body as you repeat that in your head?

May I accept myself as I am…

If you struggle to feel warmth towards yourself, perhaps imagine a loving pet or friend who has shown you unconditional love. This could be someone in the present or past. Picture them now and feel their love radiating to you.

Let's go a bit deeper, how about *May I accept my body as it is today.*

May I accept my body as it is today…

How about…*May I love my body as it is today.*

May I love my body as it is today…

Pay attention to what happens in your body as you repeat this phrase…

Allow all thoughts, feelings and sensations to arise…

Perhaps your stomach is lurching, your chest feels tight, or your shoulders are tense.

Be open to whatever arises, not judging or trying to change anything, just acknowledging it all.

Listen attentively to your body in this moment.

Now let your attention drop into wherever you feel the breath most naturally.

This could be in the tummy as it rises and falls with each in-breath and out-breath, the chest as the ribcage expands and contracts, or the nostrils…

Fully experience each in-breath and each out-breath as you centre yourself.

If uncomfortable feelings arise, say to yourself *"It is ok to feel like this"*.

If uncomfortable feelings or thoughts persist, say to yourself *"I am special. I am unique. I am enough just as I am"*. Say this to yourself as many times as you need, to provide comfort and reassurance.

When you feel like you have acknowledged your emotions and you're ready to return to daily life, remember to ground yourself before you end this practice. Take your awareness to your buttocks on the chair or on the floor. Notice how it feels to be rooted here in this moment. If you're sitting on a chair also pay attention to your feet. Notice how it feels to have all four corners of the feet firmly planted on the floor. If you're sitting cross legged pay attention to how your legs and feet feel resting on the floor.

When ready, I invite you to drop your chin to your chest, slowly open your eyes and have a good stretch. The practice is now complete.

Mindful self-compassion

Welcome to your self-compassion meditation. If you start to feel overwhelmed by emotions remember, you can always come back to the breath to anchor yourself in the present. Remember to always be kind to yourself.

Start by getting comfortable in a seated position either on a chair or on the floor. Feel free to get a blanket or cushions to ensure you're as comfortable as possible. Ensure you have an upright posture with your spine straight, shoulders nice and relaxed, feet flat on the ground or legs crossed if on the floor.

I invite you to place a hand on your heart if that feels comfortable for you. Feel free to place it back down onto your lap whenever you want to.

Now close your eyes, lower your chin towards your chest and let your attention drop to wherever you feel the breath most naturally…

This may be in your abdomen noticing your tummy rising and falling…

Or perhaps in the chest area noticing your ribcage expanding and contracting…

Or maybe you feel it more in the nostrils noticing the feeling of each in breath and out breath through your nostrils…

Wherever it feels most natural, just be with it in this moment…

Now I invite you to pay attention to your hand on your heart…

Notice the warmth of your hand resting gently on your body…

Perhaps how it moves gently along with your breath…

Now I invite you to ask yourself what is pulling for your attention right now?

Notice where you feel it in your body…

Perhaps your tummy lurches, perhaps your shoulders tense or your heart beats faster…

Perhaps other sensations arise in your body that are new to you…

Allow all sensations, thoughts and feelings to arise as you find them, welcoming everything as it arises, not trying to change anything…

Use your breath to anchor you in the present moment as each new wave of discomfort or pain appears…

Connect with how it feels in the body on each in-breath and out-breath…

Say to yourself "*It is ok to feel like this. Whatever has happened is already here. Let me feel it and welcome it as best as I can.*"

Notice what happens in your body after saying this to yourself…

Keep tuning into your breathing one breath at a time as the emotions continue to flow…

Remind yourself again, *"It is ok to feel like this"*.

Repeat this as many times as you need to, as if you were supporting a friend, holding yourself in a container of compassion.

When you feel like you have acknowledged your emotions and you're ready to return to daily life, remember to ground yourself before you end this practice. Take your awareness to your buttocks on the chair or on the floor. Notice how it feels to be rooted here in this moment. If you're sitting on a chair, also pay attention to your feet, notice how it feels to have all four corners of the feet firmly planted on the floor. If you're sitting cross legged, pay attention to how your legs and feet feel resting on the floor.

When ready, I invite you to drop your chin to your chest, slowly open your eyes and have a good stretch. The practice is now complete.

Mindful Movement

Welcome to the mindful movement practice.

Try to approach this practice with openness towards your body. Don't try to change anything or strain the body into uncomfortable positions.

Remembering to practice what feels right for you in this moment. Feel free to go at your own pace, adapting the positions to suit your body, letting the experience unfold in your own way.

If you have any medical concerns, please consult with your medical practitioner before undertaking the practice.

If you feel any discomfort during the practice, try being with it for a few breaths. If it persists, you may want to move the body with awareness until you are fully comfortable.

Try to accept whatever you experience, letting go of any judgemental thoughts that arise by taking your awareness back to the practice with kindness.

Before you start, please ensure that you are in loose, comfortable clothing with no tightness around the waist.

You may also want a pillow for your head or a bolster for your knees if you often have discomfort in your back.

We will start the practice **lying on a mat** on the floor, on a bed or sitting on a chair, if that's more comfortable for you.

Let's start by having a nice big stretch.

Stretch your arms above your head and straighten your legs as you breathe in and out.

Then position yourself in the corpse pose, lying on your back with your legs hip width apart, your toes facing outwards, feet nice and relaxed, arms by your sides a few inches from your body, palms facing upwards.

Allowing your body to relax into whatever is supporting you.

Notice how it feels to be in contact with the floor, bed or chair…

Taking a few breaths here as you sink into this position…

Take your attention to your tummy…

Notice how it feels as your tummy rises and falls to the rhythm of your own breathing…

Tune into all other sensations in your body starting with the feet, to the ankles, the calves, the thighs, the hips and buttocks, the back, the abdomen, the chest, shoulders, the arms, hands, fingers, the neck, right up to the head.

Now we'll move to a **pelvic tilt** exercise.

Lift both knees so that your feet are on the ground close to your buttocks.

Slowly and gently tilt the pelvis towards the ceiling, lifting the tailbone off the floor as your tummy contracts and the base of your spine and lower back pushes down.

Then tilt your pelvis the other way to create a curve between your lower back and whatever you are resting on.

Then once again tilt the pelvis, lifting the tailbone off the floor as your breath flows naturally, then back down onto the floor at your own pace.

Repeat this at your own pace a few times to the rhythm of your own breathing, lifting on your in-breath and dropping on your out-breath.

Now hug the **knees into the chest** and gently rock the body from side to side.

Notice how it feels in your sides, your lower back, upper back and anywhere else in the body…

Swaying from side to side to the rhythm of your own breathing.

Now bring your **knees back to the centre** while still holding onto them…

Start to slowly circle them in a clockwise direction…

Tune into your breathing so that you're breathing in on one circle and breathing out on the next…

Moving to a rhythm that suits you…

Pay attention to how it feels in your lower back, buttocks and legs…

Notice any other sensations in the body moment by moment, breath by breath.

Now repeat this move turning the knees anti-clockwise…

Once again, tune into your breathing as you circle on each in-breath and each out-breath.

Now bring the knees back to centre, feet on the floor, hip width apart.

Spending a little time here with your breathing…

Notice how your body feels after the movement.

Now keep your left knee bent as you rest your right leg on the floor.

Slowly **lift your right leg** up towards the ceiling…

If you can, lift it up to the height of your left knee. If this becomes tricky, just lift it to wherever if feels comfortable for you…

Start circling your foot in a clockwise direction for a few breaths, then in an anti-clockwise direction for a few breaths…

Sense how it feels in the whole of your right leg as the experience unfolds moment by moment…

From your buttocks, hip, thigh, calf, ankle, right up to your foot…

As the mind becomes restless, take your awareness back to the practice.

When ready, gently, slowly rest your leg back down onto the floor…

Enjoying the feeling of resting the whole of your right leg on the floor in this moment…

Spend a little time here with your breathing.

Now repeat this practice on the left side…

Lift your right knee so that your foot is resting on the floor.

When ready, gently, slowly lift your left leg up towards the ceiling…

If you can, lift it up to the height of your right knee. If this becomes tricky, just lift it to wherever if feels comfortable for you.

Start circling your foot in a clockwise direction for a few breaths, then in an anti-clockwise direction for a few breaths…

Sense how it feels in the whole your left leg as the experience unfolds moment by moment…

From your buttocks, hip, thigh, calf, ankle, right up to your foot…

Tune into your breathing in this position…

When ready, gently, slowly move your leg back down onto the floor…

Enjoying the feeling of resting the whole of your left leg on the floor in this moment.

Now let's turn your attention to your **arms**…

On your in-breath, lift both arms up towards the ceiling, shoulder width apart and palms facing each other, spreading out your fingers as wide as you can.

On an out-breath slowly let your arms drift back down again…

As your shoulders relax back onto the floor.

Repeat this, lifting your arms towards the ceiling on an in-breath…

And slowly drifting the arms back down on an out-breath.

In-breath arms slowly rise towards the ceiling…

Out-breath arms drift back down again…

Noticing where your mind is and remembering to keep tuning into your breathing…

Then gently place your arms back down onto the floor.

Now let's move to **Eye of the needle pose.**

Rest both feet on the floor close to your buttocks and hip width apart.

Rest your lower right leg on your left thigh.

Draw your left knee towards the chest.

Reach in between your legs with your right arm.

Reach around the outside of your left leg with your left arm.

Link your fingers together behind your left thigh…

Rest here for a few breaths…

You may feel a pull in your right hip and outer thigh. This is natural.

Welcome all sensations that arise here, not judging or straining…

Just be with the experience as it unfolds moment by moment…

Now repeat the posture on the other side…

Place both feet on the floor close to your buttocks and hip width apart.

Rest your lower left leg on your right thigh.

Draw your right knee towards the chest.

Reach between your legs with your left arm.

Reach around the outside of your right leg with your right arm.

Link your fingers together…

Spend a few breaths here in this position…

You may feel a pull in your left hip and outer thigh…

Perhaps one side feels tighter than the other…

Just accept whatever comes up for you…

From here move into **Cat-cow pose**…

Position yourself on your hands and knees.

Ensure your hands are directly below your shoulders and your knees are directly below your hips.

As you breathe out, gently round your back to create an arch and scoop your tailbone under…

Tilting your head downwards to look through your legs only as far as your body allows…

As you breathe in, tilt your pelvis backwards, tailbone towards the ceiling, tummy towards the floor…

Tilt the crown of your head as far as your body allows…

Continue this exercise at your own pace to the rhythm of your own breathing…

Everyone will have a different rhythm depending on the flow of your own breath.

If you notice your mind is wandering, take your awareness back to the practice…

Now let's move into **Downward facing dog pose.**

From cat-cow pose, place your feet on the floor and lift your hips.

Straighten your legs, so that the palms of your hands and your toes are touching the floor.

Take each heel to the floor one at a time as you breathe in and breathe out…

You may feel tension in your calves.

Try to approach this tension with kindness and openness…

Repetition can cause the mind to drift, so keep an eye on this, using the breath to anchor yourself back into the present moment.

Notice if you feel any tension elsewhere, such as your jaw. Move it around a little to release any tension there…

Only hold the pose for as long as your body allows – we will count for ten breaths but you can choose as many as you like…

When you are ready bend your knees and fold back into **Child's pose.**

Ensure that your knees are wide apart but with your big toes touching.

Rest your buttocks on your heels and your chest on your thighs…

Allowing your tummy to rise and fall freely.

Rest your forehead on the floor with your arms long and extended on either side of your ears, palms facing downwards…

If this is uncomfortable, you can rest your arms on either side of your body with your palms facing upwards…

Press your buttocks back on your heels to gently to ground yourself in this pose…

Enjoy the feeling of openness allowing your breath to flow naturally…

Notice any sensations that arise in your lower back, shoulders, head and anywhere else…

Rest in this position for a few breaths…

Now move to a standing position known as the **Mountain pose.**

Stand up with your arms hanging by your side, feet hip width apart, shoulders nice and relaxed.

Feel the four corners of your feet pressed into the ground.

Ensure your body weight is distributed evenly between both feet, centring it in front of your heels.

Shift your pelvis from front to back and from side to side…

Notice how that feels in your body…

Gently lift your chest, opening your heart…

Ensure that your ribs aren't sticking out and your shoulders are relaxed.

Keep your ears positioned over your shoulders…

Notice how your body may sway a little…

Try not to let boredom sink in here, remembering that if your mind wanders you can use the breath to anchor yourself back in the practice…

Sense how it feels to be grounded in this moment…

Feel the sensations in your feet, calves, thighs, buttocks…

Notice how it feels to hang your arms down by your sides freely…

Your fingers loosely hanging…

As you continue in this position for five breaths…

Now swing your arms and whole body around from your left side to your right side, keeping your feet firmly on the ground. This is a great mood enhancer!

Now finish the practice in **corpse pose** again, lying down on the floor or bed, your legs hip width apart, toes facing outwards, feet nice and relaxed, arms by your sides a few inches from your body, palms facing upwards.

Notice once again how it feels to be in contact with the floor or bed…

Take a few breaths here as you sink into this position…

Take your attention to your whole body, allowing awareness to flow from the feet, to the ankles, the calves, the thighs, the hips and buttocks, the back, the abdomen, the chest, shoulders, the arms, hands, fingers, the neck, right up to the head…

Rest here for as long as you want, enjoying the openness in your body.

Let's end the practice with a nice big stretch…

Stretch your arms above your head and straighten your legs as you breathe in and out…

Slowly sit up and congratulate yourself on taking time to nourish yourself.

Enjoy the stillness and peace you have created.

Glossary of terms

Acknowledging your thoughts – part of the mindfulness practice that involves admitting the existence of a thought, perhaps by labelling it in our heads.

Adrenaline – a hormone produced by the adrenal glands that prepares the body for 'fight or flight' mode.

Assertiveness – mindfulness of feelings, speech and actions. Communicating in a calm and positive way without coming across as aggressive or passive aggressive.

Cortisol – a hormone released by the adrenal glands to help your body to deal with stressful situations. Also regulates your metabolism and immune response.

Dopamine – an important chemical messenger in our brains involved in motivation, pleasure and reward.

Fight or flight reaction – How the body reacts to stress. It causes a surge of adrenaline and cortisol to start pumping around the body. Muscles start to tense, the heart starts pounding, blood pressure rises, sweat glands are activated, and much more besides. A lot is going on in the body as it prepares itself to fight or flee the situation.

FOBLO – Fear of being left out, of not being invited along in the first place.

FOMO – Fear of missing out.

Parasympathetic nervous system aka 'rest and digest' system – part of the nervous system which slows down and puts the brakes on our primal urge to react in fight, flight or freeze mode. It helps us to respond rather than react to the situation we're facing.

Prefrontal cortex – the part of the brain responsible for learning, thinking and reasoning. It controls our decision making and focuses our attention.

Respond or react – Calmly responding to a situation versus an emotional knee-jerk reaction.

Validate yourself – approving yourself, confirming in your head that you are enough just as you are without the need for other's approval.

Printed in Poland
by Amazon Fulfillment
Poland Sp. z o.o., Wrocław